# simple stylish
# KNITS

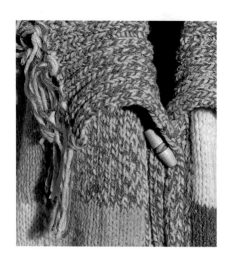

# simple stylish
# KNITS

## A fabulous collection of 24 fashionable and fun designs

### Hilary Mackin

NEW HOLLAND

This edition published in 2007

First published in 2006 by
New Holland Publishers (UK) Ltd
London · Cape Town · Sydney · Auckland

Garfield House, 86–88 Edgware Road
London W2 2EA
United Kingdom
www.newhollandpublishers.com

80 McKenzie Street
Cape Town 8001
South Africa

Level 1, Unit 4, 14 Aquatic Drive
Frenchs Forest, NSW 2086
Australia

218 Lake Road
Northcote, Auckland
New Zealand

ISBN 978 184537 891 2

Senior Editor: Clare Sayer
Production: Hazel Kirkman
Design: Isobel Gillan
Photographer: Sian Irvine
Editorial Direction: Rosemary Wilkinson

10 9 8 7 6 5 4 3 2 1

Reproduction by Pica Digital PTE Ltd
Printed and bound by Times Offset, Malaysia

# CONTENTS

# INTRODUCTION

I have always had a keen interest in crafts. I can still remember our knitting lessons at primary school where boys and girls had to participate, and being the proud owner of my first knitted dish cloth made in a thick cotton yarn. I progressed onto scarves but don't think I actually wore any of my efforts. I can remember pestering my mother as to whether I was on a knit row or a purl row, which is exactly what my daughter does to me now. I was hooked. I grew up surrounded by people who made their own

clothes, knitted, embroidered, and turned their hands to soft furnishings. My granny, mother, sister and myself used to have thrilling nights sitting round the open fire, looking at knitting magazines and choosing what to knit or make next, and longing to go out to the local wool shop to choose the yarn, and the excitement of knitting that first row – even if it took a year to complete. Our hands were never idle. The knitting would appear whilst watching the television, or any spare moment during the day. Meanwhile my father would be working on another watercolour, away from the 'clickety clack' of the knitting needles.

Knitting is such a rewarding craft and has such tremendous scope. I have always been amazed at all the different textures and colour patterns that can be achieved from one pair of knitting needles and a ball of wool. As every stitch pattern is based on the simple knit one, purl one stitches, it never ceases to amaze me that by adding variations, such as cabling, you can produce such wonderful pieces of fabric. Two garments of the same shape can look so different by just altering the yarn, stitch pattern or colourway. Knitwear is comfortable and versatile, can look smart, casual or glamorous and is suitable for all seasons.

I hope I have communicated some of my enthusiasm for this wonderful craft. Whether you are using this book as a complete beginner or as a knowledgeable knitter, I'm sure there is plenty to inspire you.

Happy clicking!

# BASIC INFORMATION

## Equipment

Knitting requires very little equipment – all you really need is a pair of needles and some yarn and you are ready to go. However, there are many different types of yarn available now and a whole range of needles to choose from, as well as some other equipment that you will find useful.

### NEEDLES

Knitting needles are available in aluminium, plastic and wood, although the larger sizes are only made in plastic and wood, as they are lighter and easier to hold.

Standard needle sizes range from 2 mm to 10 mm, although you will also find fat needles that are up to 25 mm (1 in). Generally, thick yarns are knitted using large needles and thinner yarns with small ones. The thicker the needle, the larger the stitch and the more quickly your work will progress. Needles also come in different lengths – choose ones which you find most comfortable to work with.

Cable needles are short needles which are pointed at both ends. They are used for moving stitches from one position to another when working cables.

Circular needles have two short needles which are each pointed and joined by a piece of flexible nylon which varies in length. They are much easier to handle than four double-pointed needles and are useful for neckbands or when picking up a large number of stitches around a front edge. They are ideal for any work which may be difficult to fit on a conventional needle.

## OTHER KNITTING ESSENTIALS

### Crochet hooks
These are very useful for picking up dropped stitches and working edgings on finished garments, as well as for casting off, joining seams and adding tassels.

### Stitch holder
This keeps stitches that you are not using in place until you need them. You could also use a spare needle for this.

### Tapestry needles
Blunt-ended needles with large eyes are used for sewing up items as sharp needles may split the yarn and weaken it.

### Tape measure
Use a good tape measure – ideally one that doesn't stretch, as accurate measurements are important when checking tension.

### Scissors
Have a sharp pair to hand for cutting lengths of yarn.

### Row counter
This helps you keep track of stitches and rows completed.

### Pins
Use long pins with large heads when pinning pieces together so that they will not get lost in the knitting.

## KNITTING NEEDLE CONVERSION TABLE

| Metric | British | American |
|--------|---------|----------|
| 2 mm | 14 | 00 |
| 2¼ mm | 13 | 1 |
| 2¾ mm | 12 | 2 |
| 3 mm | 11 | 2/3 |
| 3¼ mm | 10 | 3 |
| 3¾ mm | 9 | 5 |
| 4 mm | 8 | 6 |
| 4½ mm | 7 | 7 |
| 5 mm | 6 | 8 |
| 5½ mm | 5 | 8 |
| 6 mm | 4 | 9 |
| 6½ mm | 3 | 10 |
| 7 mm | 2 | 10½ |
| 7½ mm | 1 | 11 |
| 8 mm | 0 | 12 |
| 9 mm | 00 | 13 |
| 10 mm | 000 | 15 |

## Yarns

There is currently a huge selection of yarns available and choosing the right one can be daunting. You will find both natural and synthetic yarns as well as some synthetic mix yarns. Natural yarns such as wool and cotton are more expensive but they are often easier to work with. Synthetic yarns tend to be stronger.

**Wool** is easily available, long lasting and very warm. Merino sheep have the most abundant and highest quality yarn.

**Cotton** is strong, non-allergenic and easy to wash but is less elastic than wool.

**Mohair** yarn comes from Angora goats. The long silky fibres make it very warm.

**Angora** is like mohair, but softer. It is made from the hair of the Angora goat or rabbit.

**Alpaca** is less fluffy than mohair and angora; it is made from the hair of a llama-like animal.

**Cashmere** is the most expensive and luxurious of yarns, made from the fine downy hair of a special breed of goat.

**Chenille** is a velvety yarn made of tufts of cotton and synthetic yarn.

### CHOOSING YARNS

All the patterns in this book specify which yarns have been used. To ensure the item appears the same as in the pattern, you should use the yarn that the pattern recommends. If you cannot find the same yarn, choose one of a similar weight and type and knit a sample to check the tension and appearance. When buying yarn check the ball band for the dye lot number and make sure you buy balls with the same number. See page 126 for more detailed information about the yarns used.

## Getting started

### GARTER STITCH

This is the simplest of all knitted stitches and is formed by working every row in the same stitch, either knit or purl, forming the same pebbly pattern on the front and the back making it reversible. It has a sideways stretch. If every row is purled, however, you do not produce such a firm fabric.

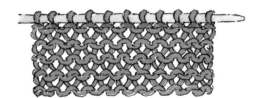

## STOCKING STITCH

This is the smoothest of all knitted stitches, and is stretchy horizontally. It is formed by working alternate rows of knitted stitches and purled stitches. The smooth, knitted side is usually called the right side. When the pattern uses the purl side as the right side, it is referred to as reverse stocking stitch.

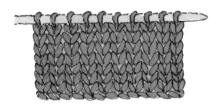

## MOSS STITCH

This stitch forms a firmer fabric than stocking stitch and is created by alternately working knit and purl stitches. Stitches that are knitted on one row will be knitted on the next row and stitches that are purled on one row will be purled on the next row. For an odd number of stitches, the instructions will be as follows; K1, *p1, k1, rep from * to end. Repeat this row.

As this stitch does not curl at the edges, it is ideal for edges. It is also reversible.

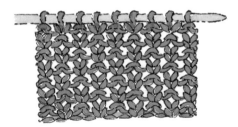

## RIB STITCH

This is formed by alternating knit and purl stitches across the same row. The knitted chain stitch forms a rib and the fabric 'shrinks' inwards and has a strong sideways stretch. It is particularly suitable for cuffs and necks and body edges to form a neat, stretchable finish. It is usually worked on smaller needles than the main body of the garment.

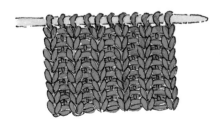

## TENSION

Making sure you have the correct tension is extremely important as it controls the shape and size of the knitted item. To make a tension swatch, knit a sample slightly larger than 10 cm (4 in) square using the same yarn, needles and stitch pattern stated in the pattern. Smooth out the sample on a flat surface, being careful not to stretch it. Using long pins, mark out the tension measurement given in the pattern, usually 10 cm (4 in). To determine the stitch tension of the knitting, count the number of stitches between the pins. Remember to include any half stitches over the width of a garment; a half stitch left uncalculated may amount to several centimetres in the final width.

To determine the length of the knitting, measure the number of rows. Place a rigid ruler or tape vertically along the fabric and count the number of rows to the centimetre. If the number of stitches given in the pattern knit up too wide it means the knitting is too loose and a size smaller needle should be used. If too small, then the knitting is too tight and a larger needle should be used.

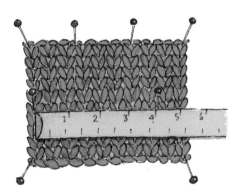

## FOLLOWING A PATTERN

Knitting patterns are written in a language all of their own. Before starting to knit any pattern, always read it right through so you are familiar with the terms.

Abbreviations are used for many of the repetitive words that occur in the instructions. See page 10 for a full list of abbreviations; any additional abbreviations will be given with each individual pattern.

Asterisks are used to indicate repetition of a sequence of stitches. For example: *k3, p1, rep from * to end. This means knit 3 stitches and purl 1 stitch to the end of the row.

| | |
|---|---|
| alt – alternate | psso – pass slipped st over |
| beg – beginning | rem – remain(ing) |
| cont – continue | rep – repeat |
| dec – decreas(e)(ing) | RH – right-hand |
| foll – following | RS – right side |
| g st – garter stitch (every row knit) | sl 1 – slip one stitch |
| inc – increas(e)(ing) | sl1-k1-psso – slip one, knit one, pass slipped stitch over the knit one |
| k – knit | |
| k1b – knit one in back of loop | st(s) – stitch(es) |
| k2tog – knit two stitches together | st st – stocking stitch, (knit row is RS, purl row is WS) |
| LH – left-hand | tbl – through back of loop(s) |
| M1 – make one by picking up loop which lies between st just worked and next st and working into the back of it | tog – together |
| | WS – wrong side |
| | wyib – with yarn in back. |
| | wyif – with yarn in front |
| p – purl | yb – yarn back |
| p1b – purl one in back of loop | yf – yarn forward |
| p2tog – purl two stitches together | yo – yarn over needle |
| | yrn – yarn round needle |
| patt – pattern | |

Brackets are used where a set of instructions need to be worked a number of times. For example: [k3, p1] 4 times. This means that the stitches within the brackets are worked 4 times in total. Brackets are also used where instructions are given for multiple sizes; in the patterns figures are given for the smallest size first and the larger sizes follow in brackets. Where the figure '0' appears in a set of brackets, no stitches or rows are to be worked in that particular size.

The instruction 'alt' usually occurs during an instruction for shaping, for example: increase 1 stitch at the end of next and every alt row until there are 10 sts. This means that, counting the next row as row 1, the increase is worked on rows 1, 3, 5, 7 etc. until the required number of stitches is reached. If the instruction reads 'increase 1 stitch at end of every alt row' then the increases are worked on rows 2, 4, 6, 8 etc.

# Care of yarns and garments

The correct after-care of all knitted garments is extremely important if they are to retain their original texture and shape. Many of the yarns available today are machine-washable and the ball band will clearly indicate where this is applicable. If in any doubt handwash in warm soapy water. Check the ball band to see whether the yarn can be dry cleaned.

When washing by hand, handle the knitting carefully and never lift the garment by the shoulders as the weight of the wet wool will drag the knitting out of shape. Squeeze out excess moisture gently without wringing. Support the overall weight with both hands and rinse thoroughly before drying to avoid matting. Spin dry for a short time only.

Never tumble dry a knitted garment. Knitting should be dried away from direct heat and laid out flat on a suitable surface. Spread the knitting out gently on a towel, and smooth out any creases. Leave until completely dry and then place over a line for final airing. Never hang knitting to drip dry. The weight of the wet fabric will pull the garment out of shape.

If a garment is properly dried it should not need pressing. If it does, check the instructions on the ball band. Some yarns may need steaming or pressing over a damp cloth. Never use a heavy hand when pressing knitted garments as this could distort the shape badly and never press ribbing.

Some yarns are prone to pilling during wear. This means that loose fibres gather into balls of fluff on the surface of the knitting. These can either be picked off, brushed or combed away, or go over the surface with a strip of sticky tape, sticky side down. Special implements can be bought for this purpose. If a snag occurs never cut it off; instead, take a blunt needle and push the snag through to the wrong side of the work. Gently tighten the yarn until the stitch is the right size and then knot the end on the wrong side.

# Basic techniques

### INCREASING AND DECREASING
Garments are most commonly shaped by increasing or decreasing the number of stitches in a row. There are many different ways of increasing and decreasing the number of stitches and each will create a slightly different appearance.

Increases and decreases are usually worked in pairs at each end of the row on the symmetrical pieces (back, sleeves etc) to give a balanced shape.

### Yarn forward increase

To make the yarn forward increase in a knit row, bring the yarn to the front, take it over the right-hand needle and knit the stitch. The complete increase creates a visible hole and is often used in lace patterns. The increase is abbreviated in knitting patterns as yf (yarn forward).

In a purl row, take the yarn over the right-hand needle to the back of the work, then under the needle to the front. The abbreviation is yrn (yarn round needle).

### Make 1 increase

Lift the yarn lying between the stitch just worked and the next stitch and place it on the left-hand needle, then knit (or purl) into the back of this loop. This increase is abbreviated as M1 (make 1).

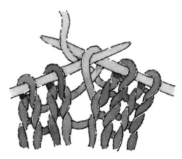

### Slip stitch decrease

Slip the next stitch onto the right-hand needle without knitting it, then knit the next stitch. Lift the slipped stitch over the knitted stitch and drop it off the needle. This decrease is abbreviated as sl 1, k1, psso (on right side) and sl 1, p1, psso (on wrong side).

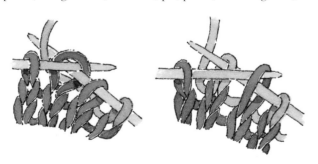

### Working two stitches together

This decrease is worked simply by inserting the right-hand needle through two stitches instead of one and then knitting them together as one stitch. On a purl row, insert the needle purlwise through the two stitches and purl in the usual way. This decrease is abbreviated as k2tog (right side) or p2tog (wrong side).

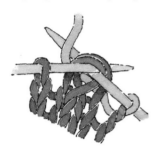

### CHANGING COLOUR

To join in a new colour at the start of a row, insert the needle into the first stitch and using the new colour, make a loop over the right-hand needle. Pull through to complete the stitch and continue to the end of the row. Carry the yarn up the side of the work for narrow stripes but break it off and rejoin it for wider stripes.

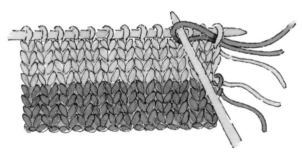

Where colours are worked in blocks, it is best to use a separate ball of yarn for each section. Twist the yarns over each other at the junction of each colour change to avoid a hole forming. When the colour change occurs in vertical lines, cross the yarns on both knit and purl rows. When the colour change is on a slanting line, the yarns need to be crossed on alternate rows.

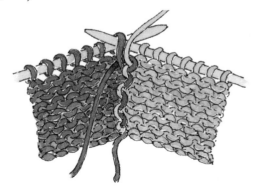

## MAKING HORIZONTAL BUTTONHOLES

These may be worked on the main fabric or on a separate narrow band.

Work to the position of the buttonhole and cast off the number of stitches required for the width of the button and knit to the end of the row. Work to within one stitch of the cast-off stitches and knit twice into it. Then cast on one stitch less than was cast off and work to the end of the row.

Once the garment is complete, you can finish off the buttonhole by working round it in buttonhole stitch.

## MAKING UP GARMENTS

Even the simplest garments require neat and careful making up so it is worth spending some time at the final stages for professional looking garments.

Before you begin joining pieces together, weave in any loose ends of yarn into a seam edge. Cover the pieces with a damp cloth and press gently with a steam iron – this will make them easier to join.

### Joining seams

There are various different ways of sewing knitted pieces together but the garments in this book use the backstitch seam method. Use a blunt-ended needle.

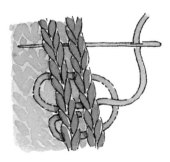

Place the pieces to be joined together with their right sides facing inwards, ensuring that the stitches and rows are aligned. Sewing into the centre of each stitch, bring the needle out one stitch in from the edge, insert the needle one stitch back and bring the needle out one stitch ahead of the emerging thread. Sew a few mm (¼ in) in from the edge of the knitting.

### Joining sleeves

The top of the sleeve and the armhole into which it is set can often be different shapes so care needs to be taken when inserting the sleeves. Once the shoulder seams have been joined, fold the sleeve in half lengthways. Mark the centre of the top of the sleeve and the midway points between the centre and the underarm with pins.

On the main body of the garment, mark the centre of the shoulder join and midway points from that point and the underarm with pins. With right sides together, pin the sleeve into the armhole, matching up the marker pins. Using a backstitch seam, sew the sleeve seam on the inside.

### Collars

Collars can either be knitted in by first picking up stitches around the neck edge or made separately and sewn on.

For a picked-up collar, join one shoulder as indicated on pattern. Divide the neck edge into sections and mark with pins to space the picked-up stitches evenly, then calculate how many stitches will be needed for each section. When working a non-reversible stitch such as stocking stitch remember to pick up the stitches from the correct side to ensure that the pattern is on the right side when the collar is turned over.

For a sewn-on collar, divide the neck edge and the inner collar edge into the same number of equal sections and mark them with a pin. With the right side of the collar facing the wrong side of the garment, pin the two edges together and sew.

### Zips

Always insert an open-ended zip with the fastener closed to ensure that both sides match.

Pin the zip in position, taking care not to stretch the knitting. Use an ordinary sewing needle and matching thread. With the right side of the work facing, sew in the zip with a back-stitch seam keeping as close to the knitted edge as possible. Always work from top to bottom and take care not to cover the zip teeth. Slip stitch down the zip edges on the inside afterwards.

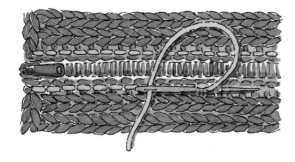

## Decorative edges
These may be used to trim garments. They can be made separately and sewn on afterwards or knitted as part of the garment. Knit a length as indicated on the pattern, then with right side of edging to right side of garment, divide into equal sections and pin, sew in position using a back stitch. Allow extra ease for any curves on the main garment, so that the edging lies flat after sewing.

## Making tassels
Cut out a piece of card the same length that you want the tassel to be. Wind yarn around the card to the required thickness. Thread a needle with yarn and pull it under the strands at the top of the card. Tie securely, leaving a long end. Using a sharp pair of scissors, cut through the yarn at the other end of the card. Wind the long end of yarn around the tassel several times about 1.5 cm (¾ in) from the top and secure by pushing the needle up through the middle of the tassel.

## Fringing
Cut the yarn into the required lengths – just over twice the required finished length of the fringe. Fold in half and, with the wrong side of the fabric facing you, draw a loop through the edge stitch using a crochet hook. Then draw the loose ends of the strands through this loop and pull down tightly to form a knot. Repeat at regular intervals.

## Sewn-on pockets
Use a slip stitch seam to apply the pocket, taking care to keep the line of the pocket and main fabric straight. A useful tip is to use a fine knitting needle, pointed at both ends, to pick up every alternate stitch along the line of the main fabric, then catch one stitch from the edge of the pocket and one stitch from the needle alternately. Make sure that the lower edge of the pocket lies in a straight line across a row of the main fabric.

## ADAPTING PATTERNS
Sometimes it may be necessary to alter a pattern to suit your own body measurements. Working with the tension quoted on the pattern, calculate the amendments necessary to the stitches and rows and mark the alterations on the pattern.

# CLASSIC

This chapter is full of timeless classics knitted in wonderful modern yarns, with features such as loop stitch, fringing and easy stitches. Wear with jeans for a casual look or be comfortably smart. There are ideas here for classic styling that would be ideal for any occasion – the office, out to lunch, shopping or days out. Win admiring glances when you wear any of the easy and quick to knit coats. The shawl-collared coat on page 26 looks fabulous when teamed with the striped sweater on page 32 – the colours complement each other perfectly.

*This stylish coat is knitted in stocking stitch with garter stitch borders. It is surprisingly quick and easy to knit.*

# LONG ASYMMETRICAL COAT

★★☆ EASY

 *Although this is a very easy garment to knit, the asymmetrical shaping requires accurate row counting.*

## HELPFUL HINT

- To make sure the fronts are even, lay the garment out before sewing the front band in position. Sew with a back stitch, stretching the front bands slightly around the front edges above button fastenings.

## MEASUREMENTS

### To fit bust

| 81 | 86 | 91 | 97 | 102 | 107 | cm |
|----|----|----|----|-----|-----|----|
| 32 | 34 | 36 | 38 | 40 | 42 | in |

### Actual width

| 115 | 120 | 125 | 130 | 135 | 140 | cm |
|-----|-----|-----|-----|-----|-----|----|
| 45¼ | 47¼ | 49½ | 51¼ | 53¼ | 55¼ | in |

### Actual length

| 98 | 100 | 102 | 104 | 106 | 109 | cm |
|----|-----|-----|-----|-----|-----|----|
| 30½ | 39½ | 40 | 41 | 41¼ | 43 | in |

### Actual sleeve seam

| 43 | 46 | 46 | 46 | 46 | 47 | cm |
|----|----|----|----|----|----|----|
| 17 | 18 | 18 | 18 | 18 | 18½ | in |

*In the instructions figures are given for the smallest size first; larger sizes follow in brackets. Where only one set of figures is given this applies to all sizes.*

## MATERIALS

- 12 (13:14:15:16:17) × 100 g balls of Rowan Big Wool in Tremble 035 (MC)
- 3 × 100 g balls of Rowan Yorkshire Tweed Chunky in Stout 554 (C)
- Pair each of 7 mm and 12 mm needles
- Buckle, 6 cm (2½ in) in diameter
- Button

## TENSION

8 sts and 11 rows to 10 cm (4 in) measured over stocking stitch using MC and 12 mm needles.

## ABBREVIATIONS

*See page 10.*

# COAT

## BACK

With 7 mm needles and C, cast on 65 (68:71:73:76:79) sts and knit 7 rows.

**Dec row:** (k1, k2tog) 6 (6:7:6:6:7) times, (k2, k2tog) 7 (7:7:9:9:9) times, (k1, k2tog) 6 (7:7:6:7:7) times, k1. [46 (48:50:52:54:56) sts.]

Change to 12 mm needles and MC.

Cont in st st, beg with a knit row, work 104 (106:108:110:112:116) rows, ending with a WS row.

Work measures approximately 98 (100:102:104:106:109) cm (38½ (39½:40:41:41¾:43) in) from beg.

### Shape shoulder

Cast off 5 (5:5:5:6:6) sts at beg of the next 2 rows, 5 (5:6:6:6:6) sts on the next 2 rows, 5 (6:6:6:6:7) sts on the next 2 rows. Cast off rem 16 (16:16:18:18:18) sts.

### LEFT FRONT

With 7 mm needles and C, cast on 33 (34:35:37:38:39) sts and knit 7 rows.
**Dec row:** K2 (3:3:3:3:4), (k2tog, k1) 9 (9:9:10:10:10) times, k2tog, k2 (2:3:2:3:3). [23 (24:25:26:27:28) sts.]
Change to 12 mm needles and MC. Cont in st st beg with a knit row. Work 5 (7:9:5:7:9) rows, then inc 1 st at beg (front edge) on the next and at this same edge on the 0 (0:0:3:3:3) foll 8th rows [24 (25:26:30:31:32) sts], then on the 9 (9:9:6:6:6) foll 6th rows, 33 (34:35:36:37:38) sts. Work 6 rows. Place a marker at front edge on the last row. Dec 1 st at front edge on the next and 12 (12:12:13:13:13) foll alt rows, then on the 5 foll 4th rows. [15 (16:17:17:18:19) sts.] Work 3 (3:5:3:3:5) rows, ending with a WS row.

### Shape shoulder

Cast off 5 (5:5:5:6:6) sts at beg of the next row, 5 (5:6:6:6:6) sts on the foll alt row. Work 1 row. Cast off rem 5 (6:6:6:6:7) sts.

### RIGHT FRONT

Work as given for Left Front, reversing shapings.

### SLEEVES (MAKE 2)

With 7 mm needles and C, cast on 38 (38:41:41:44:44) sts and knit 7 rows.
**Dec row:** K2, (k1, k2tog) 11 (11:12:12:13:13) times, k3. [27 (27:29:29:31:31) sts.]
Change to 12 mm needles and MC. Cont in st st beg with a knit row, at the same time inc 1 st at both ends of the 13th (13th:9th:9th: 7th:7th) and 2 (2:3:3:4:4) foll 14th (14th: 10th:10th:8th:8th) rows.
[33 (33:37:37:41:41) sts.] Cont straight until Sleeve measures 43 (43:46:46:46:47) cm (17 (18:18:18:18:18½) in) from beg, ending with a WS row.

### Shape sleeve top

Cast off 6 (6:7:7:8:8) sts at beg of the next 4 rows. Cast off rem 9 sts.

### POCKETS (MAKE 2)

With 7 mm needles and C, cast on 20 sts. Knit 1 row.
**Dec row:** K1, (k1, k2tog) 6 times, k1. [14 sts.]
Change to 12 mm needles and MC. Cont in st st beg with a knit row. Work 15 rows.
**Inc row:** WS. P1, (p2, M1) 6 times, p1. [20 sts.]
Change to 7 mm needles and C. Knit 8 rows. Cast off.

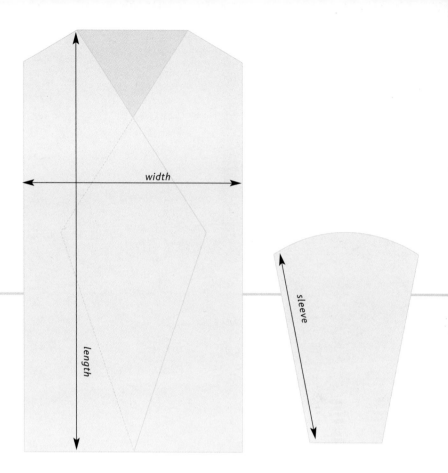

## POCKET SIDES (MAKE 2)

With right side facing, 7 mm needles and C, knit up 20 sts along one side edge of pocket. Knit 1 row. Cast off. Rep on other side.

## TIES

### Right front

With 7 mm needles and C, cast on 26 sts. Knit 7 rows. Cast off.

### Left front

With 7 mm needles and C, cast on 10 sts. Knit 7 rows. Cast off.

## TO MAKE UP

Join shoulders.

### Front band

With 7 mm needles and C, cast on 7 sts.
**Next row:** Sl 1, k5, k1b.
Rep this row until band fits all round fronts and back neck edge. Cast off.
Sew on Front Band.
Attach Right Front Tie, positioning top corner to marker on Right Front, and under Front Band.
Position top of Left Front Tie, 10 (11:12:13:14:15) cm (4 (4½:4¾:5:5½:6) in) in from side seam in line with marker on Left Front, sew down top and bottom for 3 cm (1¼ in) and short end of Tie nearest side seam.

To cover the buckle, wrap the same yarn as used for the ties around the buckle and secure with a buttonhole stitch. Wrap other end of tie around inner stem of Buckle and secure. Sew a loop to edge of Front Band on Left Front so that the top of loop lies at marker. Sew a button to wrong side of Right Front to correspond with loop.

Sew pockets neatly to Fronts, positioning the bottom of the pocket 33 (35:36:38:40:42) cm (13 (13¾:14:15:15¾:16½) in) up from cast-on edge and 3 cm (1¼ in) in from side seam. Fold sleeves in half lengthways, place folds to shoulder seams and sew sleeves in position approximately 22 (22:24:24:25:25) cm (8¾ (8¾:9½:9½:9¾:9¾) in) from top of shoulder. Join side and sleeve seams. Pin out garment to the measurement given on page 16. Cover with damp cloths and leave until dry.

*Although this is a large garment it can be knitted up very quickly. The attractive basketweave fabric is really easy to create and the large sailor collar and tassels are the perfect details. To top it all you can knit a matching beret.*

# BASKETWEAVE COAT AND HAT

★★☆ EASY

*Some experience is needed to create the basketweave fabric.*

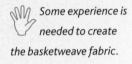

*This garment requires neat making up.*

## MEASUREMENTS

**To fit bust**

| 81–86 | 91–97 | 102–107 | 112–117 | 122–127 | cm |
|-------|-------|---------|---------|---------|-----|
| 32–34 | 36–38 | 40–42 | 44–46 | 48–50 | in |

**Actual width**

| 110 | 123 | 130 | 143 | 150 | cm |
|-----|-----|-----|-----|-----|-----|
| 43½ | 48½ | 51¼ | 56¼ | 59 | in |

**Actual length**

| 102 | 107 | 112 | 117 | 122 | cm |
|-----|-----|-----|-----|-----|-----|
| 40 | 42 | 44 | 46 | 48 | in |

**Actual sleeve seam**

| 42 | 42 | 42 | 44 | 44 | cm |
|----|----|----|----|----|-----|
| 16½ | 16½ | 16½ | 17½ | 17½ | in |

*In the instructions figures are given for the smallest size first; larger sizes follow in brackets. Where only one set of figures is given this applies to all sizes.*

## MATERIALS

**For the coat**

- 18 (19:20:21:22) × 100 g balls of Sirdar Bigga in Blue Suede 694
- Pair of 15 mm needles
- Stitch holders
- 3 buttons

**For the hat**

- 2 × 100 g balls of Sirdar Bigga in Blue Suede 694
- Pair of 15 mm needles

## TENSION

6 sts and 9 rows to 10 cm (4 in) measured over stocking stitch using 15 mm needles.

## ABBREVIATIONS

*See page 10.*

# COAT

## BACK

With 15 mm needles cast on 33 (37:39:43:45) sts.

**Row 1:** RS. *K1, p1; rep from * to last st, k1.

**Row 2:** *P1, k1; rep from * to last st, p1.

These 2 rows form the rib. Work 4 more rows in rib.

Cont in main patt as follows:

**Row 1:** RS. Knit.

**Row 2:** K3 (5:2:4:5), *p3, k5; rep from * to last 6 (8:5:7:8) sts, p3, k3 (5:2:4:5).

**Row 3:** P3 (5:2:4:5), *k3, p5; rep from * to last 6 (8:5:7:8) sts, k3, p3 (5:2:4:5).

**Row 4:** As Row 2.

**Row 5:** Knit.

**Row 6:** P2 (0:1:3:0), k5 (1:5:5:1), *p3, k5; rep from * to last 10 (4:9:11:4) sts, p3, k5 (1:5:5:1), p2 (0:1:3:0).

**Row 7:** K2 (0:1:3:0), p5 (1:5:5:1), *k3, p5; rep from * to last 10 (4:9:11:4) sts, k3, p5 (1:5:5:1), k2 (0:1:3:0).

**Row 8:** As Row 6.

These 8 rows form the main patt and are repeated throughout.

Cont in patt until work measures 102 (107:112:117:122) cm (40 (42:44:46:48) in) from beg, ending with a WS row.

### Shape shoulders

Cast off 6 (7:7:8:8) sts at beg of the next 2 rows. [21 (23:25:27:29) sts.]
Cast off 6 (7:8:8:9) sts at beg of the next 2 rows. Cast off rem 9 (9:9:11:11) sts.

### POCKET LININGS (MAKE 2)

With 15 mm needles and using the thumb method, cast on 11 sts. Work 16 rows in st st beg with a knit row. Leave sts on a st holder.

### LEFT FRONT

With 15 mm needles cast on 20 (22:24:26:28) sts and work 6 rows in rib as follows:
**Row 1:** RS. *K1, p1; rep from * to last 2 sts, k1, k1b.
**Row 2:** Sl 1, *p1, k1; rep from * to last st, p1. Work 4 more rows in rib.
Cont in main patt as follows:
**Row 1:** RS. Knit to the last 4 sts, k1, p1, k1, k1b (these last 4 sts form the front band).
**Row 2:** Sl 1, p1, k1, p1 (these 4 sts form the front band), p0 (0:2:2:3), k2 (2:5:5:5), p3, k5, p3, k3 (5:2:4:5).
**Row 3:** P3 (5:2:4:5), k3, p5, k3, p2 (2:5:5:5), k0 (0:2:2:3), k1, p1, k1, k1b.
**Row 4:** As Row 2.

**Row 5:** Knit to the last 4 sts, k1, p1, k1, k1b.
**Row 6:** Sl 1, p1, k1, p1, k0 (0:3:3:4), p1 (1:3:3:3), k5, p3, k5, p2 (3:1:3:3), k0 (1:0:0:1).
**Row 7:** P0 (3:0:0:1), k2 (3:1:3:3), p5, k3, p5, k1 (1:3:3:3), p0 (0:3:3:4), k1, p1, k1, k1b.
**Row 8:** As Row 6.
Cont straight in patt as now set until work measures 53 (58:62:66:70) cm (21 (23:24½:26:27½) in) from beg, ending with a WS row.

### Place pocket

Patt 3 (4:5:6:7), slip the next 11 sts on a st holder and patt across 11 sts from one st holder for pocket lining, patt 2 (3:4:5:6), k1, p1, k1, k1b.
Cont straight in patt on these sts until Front measures 22 (24:26:28:30) rows shorter than Back to beg of shoulder shaping, ending with a WS row. **

### Work rib for collar

**Row 1:** Patt to last 7 sts, work 2tog, k1, M1, rib to end.
**Row 2:** Sl 1, rib 4, M1, p1, patt to end.
**Row 3:** Patt to last 9 sts, work 2tog, k1, M1, rib to end.
**Row 4:** Sl 1, rib 6, M1, p1, patt to end.
**Row 5:** Patt to last 11 sts, work 2tog, k1, M1, rib to end.
**Row 6:** Sl 1, rib 8, M1, p1, patt to end.

**Row 7:** Patt to last 13 sts, work 2tog, k1, M1, rib to end.

**Row 8:** Sl 1, rib 10, M1, p1, patt to end.

**Row 9:** Patt to last 15 sts, work 2tog, k1, M1, rib to end.

**Row 10:** Sl 1, rib 12, M1, p1, patt to end. [25 (27:29:31:33) sts.]

*2nd, 3rd, 4th and 5th sizes*

**Row 11:** Patt to last 17 sts, work 2tog, k1, M1, rib to end.

**Row 12:** Sl 1, rib 14, M1, p1, patt to end. [(28:30:32:34) sts.]

*3rd, 4th and 5th sizes*

**Row 13:** Patt to last 19 sts, work 2tog, k1, M1, rib to end.

**Row 14:** Sl 1, rib 16, M1, p1, patt to end. [(31:33:35) sts.]

*4th and 5th sizes*

**Row 15:** Patt to last 21 sts, work 2tog, k1, M1, rib to end.

**Row 16:** Sl 1, rib 18, M1, p1, patt to end. [(34:36) sts.]

*5th size*

**Row 17:** Patt to last 23 sts, work2tog, k1, M1, rib to end.

**Row 18:** Sl 1, rib 20, M1, p1, patt to end. [37 sts.]

*All sizes*

Cont straight in patt as now set until work measures same as Back to beg of shoulder shaping, ending with a WS row.

## Shape shoulder

Cast off 6 (7:7:8:8) sts at beg of the next row [19 (21:24:26:29) sts], 6 (7:8:8:9) sts on the foll alt row ending with a RS row. Leave rem 13 (14:16:18:20) sts on a st holder.

Place markers for 3 buttons on front band, the first to come 41 (44:48:52:56) cm (16 (17½:19:20½:22) in) up from cast-on edge, the last 3 cm (1¼ in) down from beg of rib for collar and the remaining spaced evenly between.

## RIGHT FRONT

With 15 mm needles cast on 20 (22:24:26:28) sts and work 6 rows in rib as follows:

**Row 1:** RS. Sl 1, *k1, p1; rep from * to last st, k1.

**Row 2:** *P1, k1; rep from * to last 2 sts, p1, k1b. Cont in main patt placing patt as follows:

**Row 1:** Sl 1, k1, p1, k1, knit to end.

**Row 2:** K3 (5:2:4:5), p3, k5, p3, k2 (2:5:5:5), p0 (0:2:2:3), p1, k1, p1, k1b.

**Row 3:** Sl 1, k1, p1, k1, k0 (0:2:2:3), p2 (2:5:5:5), k3, p5, k3, p3 (5:2:4:5).

**Row 4:** As Row 2.

**Row 5:** Sl 1, k1, p1, k1, knit to end.

**Row 6:** K0 (1:0:0:1), p2 (3:1:3:3), k5, p3, k5, p1 (1:3:3:3), k0 (0:3:3:4), p1, k1, p1, k1b.

**Row 7:** Sl 1, k1, p1, k1, p0 (0:3:3:4), k1 (1:3:3:3), p5, k3, p5, k2 (3:1:3:3), p0 (1:0:0:1).

**Row 8:** As Row 6.

Cont straight in patt as now set making buttonholes in front band to correspond with markers on Left Front as follows:

### Buttonhole row – right side
Sl 1, k1, yo, k2tog, patt to end.
Place pocket when work measures 53 (58:62:66:70) cm (21 (23:24½:26:27½) in) from beg, ending with a WS row.

### Place pocket
**Next row:** Sl 1, k1, p1, k1, patt 2 (3:4:5:6), sl the next 11 sts on a st holder and patt across 11 sts from rem pocket st holder, patt rem 3 (4:5:6:7) sts.
Cont straight in patt on these sts working as given for Left Front to **.

### Work rib for collar
**Row 1:** RS. Sl 1, rib 3, M1, k1, work 2tog, patt to end.
**Row 2:** Patt to last 6 sts, p1, M1, rib 4, k1b.
Complete as given for Left Front, reversing shapings.

## SLEEVES (MAKE 2)
With 15 mm needles cast on 21 (21:23:23:25) sts and work 6 rows in rib as given for Back welt.
Cont in main patt placing patt as follows:
**Row 1:** RS. Knit.

**Row 2:** K1 (1:2:2:3), (p3, k5) twice, p3, k1 (1:2:2:3).
**Row 3:** P1 (1:2:2:3), (k3, p5) twice, k3, p1 (1:2:2:3).
Cont in patt as given for Back as now set, at the same time inc 1 st at both ends of the 13th (13th:7th:7th:7th) and 1 (1:2:2:3) foll 13th (13th:8th:8th:7th) rows. [25 (25:29:29:33) sts.]
Cont straight in patt until Sleeve measures 42 (42:42:44:44) cm (16½ (16½:16½:17½:17½) in) from beg, ending with a WS row.

### Shape sleeve top
Cast off 5 (5:6:6:6) sts at beg of the next 2 rows, [15 (15:17:17:21) sts], 5 (5:6:6:7) sts at beg of the next 2 rows. Cast off rem 5 (5:5:5:7) sts.

## BACK COLLAR
Join shoulders.
**Next row:** Beg at front edge st on Right Front Collar, sl 1, rib 12 (13:15:17:19), M1, knit up 9 (9:9:11:11) sts from back neck, starting at neck edge on Left Front Collar, M1, rib 12 (13:15:17:19), k1b. [37 (39:43:49:53) sts.]
Cont in rib until Back Collar measures 30 cm (11¾ in), ending with a WS row. Cast off ribwise.

## POCKET BORDERS (MAKE 2)
With RS facing and 15 mm needles, rib across 11 sts from one pocket top. Rib 2 more rows. Cast off ribwise.

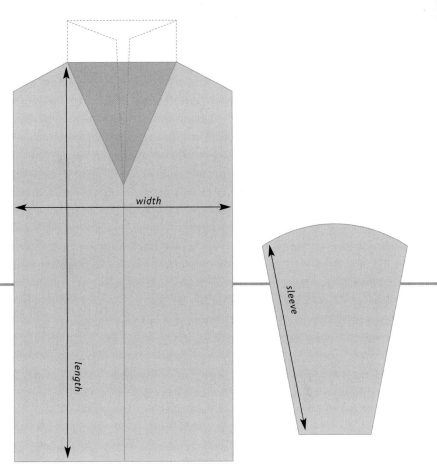

## TO MAKE UP

Sew pocket linings and borders in position.
Sew sleeves in position for approximately
21 (21:24:24:28) cm (8¼ (8¼:9½:9½:11) in)
from top of shoulder. Join side and sleeve seams.
For each tassel, cut 3 stands of yarn each
approximately 28 cm (11 in), see Making
Tassels, page 13. Tie in tassels to cast-off edge
on Collar approximately 4 sts apart. Trim as
required so that each tassel measures 12 cm
(4¾ in). Sew on buttons.
Cover with damp cloths and leave until dry.

# HAT

With 15 mm needles, cast on 31 sts.
**Row 1:** RS. *P1, k1; rep from * to last st, p1.
**Row 2:** *K1, p1; rep from * to last st, k1.
**Row 3:** As row 1.
**Inc row:** K3, *M1, k2; rep from * 13 times,
M1, k2. [45 sts.]
Cont in patt as follows:
**Row 1:** RS. Knit.
**Row 2:** K5, *p3, k5; rep from * to end.
**Row 3:** P5, *k3, p5; rep from * to end.
**Row 4:** As Row 2.
**Row 5:** Knit.
**Row 6:** K1, *p3, k5; rep from * end last rep k1.
**Row 7:** P1, *k3, p5; rep from * end last rep p1.
**Row 8:** As Row 6.
Knit 2 rows.

### Shape crown
**Row 1 dec:** RS. *Sl 1, k1, psso, k1, k2tog, k4;
rep from * 5 times. [35 sts.]
Purl 1 row.
**Row 2 dec:** *Sl 1, k1, psso, k1, k2tog, k2; rep
from * 5 times. [25 sts.]
Purl 1 row.
**Row 3 dec:** *Sl 1, k1, psso, k1, k2tog; rep
from * 5 times. [15 sts.]
Purl 1 row.
**Row 4 dec:** *K2tog; rep from * 7 times, k1.
[8 sts.]
Purl 1 row.
**Row 5 dec:** *K2tog; rep from * 4 times. [4 sts.]
Break yarn and thread through sts, pull up
tightly and secure.
Join back seam.
Make a tassel as given for Collar and tie in to
centre of crown (see Making Tassels, page 13).

*This interesting yarn together with an easy slip stitch pattern gives extra appeal to this long line coat, which is perfect for wearing over a pair of casual trousers for a warm yet elegant look.*

# LONG SHAWL-COLLARED COAT

★★☆ EASY

 The slip stitch pattern used to make this coat is very easy to work.

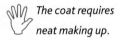 Some experience is need to do the shaping and collar on this garment.

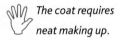 The coat requires neat making up.

## MEASUREMENTS

**To fit bust**

| | | | | | |
|---|---|---|---|---|---|
| 81 | 86 | 91 | 97 | 102 | cm |
| 32 | 34 | 36 | 38 | 40 | in |

**Actual width**

| | | | | | |
|---|---|---|---|---|---|
| 95 | 100 | 104 | 113 | 117 | cm |
| 37½ | 39½ | 41 | 44½ | 46 | in |

**Actual length**

| | | | | | |
|---|---|---|---|---|---|
| 90 | 90 | 92 | 92 | 94 | cm |
| 35½ | 35½ | 36¼ | 36¼ | 37 | in |

**Actual sleeve seam**

46 cm

18 in

*In the instructions figures are given for the smallest size first; larger sizes follow in brackets. Where only one set of figures is given this applies to all sizes.*

## MATERIALS

- 14 (14:15:15:16) × 100 g balls of Rowan Ribbon Twist in Ribble 111
- Pair of 12 mm needles
- Stitch holders
- 3 buttons

## TENSION

9 sts and 11 rows to 10 cm (4 in) measured over pattern using 12 mm needles.

## ABBREVIATIONS

*See page 10.*

# COAT

## BACK

With 12 mm needles cast on 51 (55:59:63:67) sts.

**Foundation row:** WS. *K3, p1; rep from * to last 3 sts, k3.

**Row 1:** *P3, k1 winding yarn twice round needle; rep from * to last 3 sts, p3.

**Row 2:** *K3, sl 1 purlwise wyif and dropping extra loop, yb; rep from * to last 3 sts, k3.

Rows 1 and 2 form the patt. Cont in patt dec 1 st at each end of the 17th and 5 (2:6:6:4) foll 8th (8th:6th:6th:6th) rows [39 (49:45:49:57) sts], then on the 0 (4:1:1:4) foll 0 (6th:4th:4th:4th) rows [39 (41:43:47:49) sts], then inc 1 st at each end of the next and foll 6th row.

[43 (45:47:51:53) sts.]

Work 10 rows straight, ending with a WS row.

[74 rows – work measures approximately 67 cm (26½ in) from beg.]

## Shape armholes

Cast off 2 (2:3:3:4) sts at beg of the next 2 rows [39 (41:41:45:45) sts], then dec 1 st at each end of the next 3 rows [33 (35:35:39:39) sts], then on the 2 foll alt

rows [29 (31:31:35:35) sts]. Work a further 15 (15:17:17:19) patt rows, ending with a WS row.

## Shape shoulders and back neck

Cast off 4 (4:4:5:5) sts at beg of the next row, work in patt until there are 5 (6:6:6:6) sts on RH needle after cast-off, turn and leave rem sts on a st holder. Work on these sts for first side.

Dec 1 st at neck edge on the next row. Cast off rem 4 (5:5:5:5) sts.

With RS facing, cast off the centre 11 (11:11:13:13) sts and work in patt to end. Complete this side to match first side, reversing shapings.

## POCKET LININGS (MAKE 2)

With 12 mm needles cast on 11 sts. Cont in st st beg with a knit row. Work 14 rows and leave on a st holder.

## LEFT FRONT

With 12 mm needles cast on 30 (34:36:38:40) sts.
Cont in patt as follows:

**Foundation row:** WS. (P1, k1) 3 times, p1, k3 (3:5:3:5), p1, *k3, p1; rep from * to last 3 sts, k3.

**Row 1:** *P3, k1 winding yarn twice round needle; rep from * to last 10 (10:12:10:12) sts, p3 (3:5:3:5), (k1, p1) 3 times, k1.

**Row 2:** (P1, k1) 3 times, p1, k3 (3:5:3:5), p1, *k3, sl 1 purlwise wyif and dropping extra loop, yb; rep from * to last 3 sts, k3.

Cont in patt as Back, dec 1 st at side edge on the 17th and 3 (2:4:4:4) foll 8th (8th:6th:6th:6th) rows [26 (31:31:33:35) sts], then on the 0 (2:0:0:1) foll 0 (6th:0:0:4th) rows [26 (29:31:33:34) sts]. Work 5 (1:5:5:1) rows, ending with WS row.

## Place pocket

**Next row:** Patt 0 (0:2:2:0) tog, patt 4 (5:4:5:8) sts, rib across next 11 sts for pocket top, turn and work 2 rows in rib on these 11 sts, cast off these 11 sts. Break yarn. With RS facing, rejoin yarn to one pocket lining, cont in patt across these sts then patt 4 (6:7:7:8), rib 7. [26 (29:30:32:34) sts.]

Work 1 (3:5:5:1) rows. Dec 1 st at side edge on the next and 1 (1:1:1:2) foll 8th (6th:4th:4th:4th) row [24 (27:28:30:31) sts], then inc 1 st at side edge on the next and foll 6th row. [26 (29:30:32:33) sts.]

Work 4 rows straight, ending with a WS row. Place marker at front edge on last row. ***

## Shape neck and collar

**Row 1:** Patt to last 10 sts, patt 3tog, M1, rib to end. [25 (28:29:31:32) sts.]

**Row 2:** Rib 8, patt to end.

**Row 3:** Patt to last 8 sts, M1, rib to end. [26 (29:30:32:33) sts.]

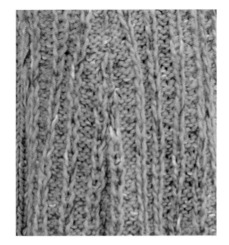

**Row 4:** Rib 9, patt to end.
**Row 5:** Patt to last 9 sts, M1, rib to end.
[27 (30:31:33:34) sts.]
**Row 6:** Rib 10, patt to end.

### Shape armhole

**Row 7:** Cast off 2 (2:3:3:4) sts at beg of the next row, patt to last 13 sts, patt 3tog, M1, rib to end. [24 (27:27:29:29) sts.]
**Row 8:** Rib 11, patt to end.
**Row 9:** Patt 2tog, patt to last 11 sts, M1, rib to end. [24 (27:27:29:29) sts.]
**Row 10:** Rib 12, patt to last 2 sts, patt 2tog.
**Row 11:** Patt 2tog, patt to last 12 sts, M1, rib to end. [23 (26:26:28:28) sts.]
**Row 12:** Rib 13, patt to end.
*1st size*
**Row 13:** Patt 2tog, patt to last 13 sts, M1, rib to end. [23 sts.]
**Row 14:** Rib 14, patt to end.
*2nd, 3rd, 4th and 5th sizes*
**Row 13:** Patt 2tog, patt to last 16 sts, patt 3tog, M1, rib to end. [(24:24:26:26) sts.]
**Row 14:** Rib 14, patt to end.
*All sizes*
**Row 15:** Patt 2tog, patt to last 14 sts, M1, rib to end.
**Rows 16, 18 and 20:** In patt as set.
**Row 17:** Patt to last 15 sts, M1, rib to end.
**Row 19:** Patt to last 16 sts, M1, rib to end.
**Row 21:** Patt to last 17 sts, M1, rib to end.
[26 (27:27:29:29) sts.]

*3rd, 4th and 5th sizes*
**Row 22:** In patt as set.
**Row 23:** Patt to last 18 sts, M1, rib to end.
[(28:30:30) sts.]
*5th size*
**Row 24:** In patt as set.
**Row 25:** Patt to last 19 sts, M1, rib to end.
[31 sts.]
*All sizes*
Work 9 rows as set, ending at side edge.
[26 (27:28:30:31) sts.]

### Shape shoulder

Cast off 4 (4:4:5:5) sts at beg of the next row, cast off 4 (5:5:5:5) sts on the foll alt row.
[18 (18:19:20:21) sts.]
**Next row:** Rib 15 (15:16:17:18) sts, slip next st onto RH needle and take yarn to opposite side of work between needle, slip the same st back onto LH needle (referred to as wrap 1), turn.
**Next row:** In rib.
**Next row:** Rib 13 (13:14:15:16), wrap 1, turn.
**Next row:** In rib.
**Next row:** Rib 11 (11:12:13:14), wrap 1, turn.
Cont without shaping until collar is of sufficient length to go halfway across back of neck, ending with a WS row. Cast off.
Mark the positions of 3 buttons, the first in line with cast-off edge on pocket top, the last 4 rows down from marker and the remainder spaced between.

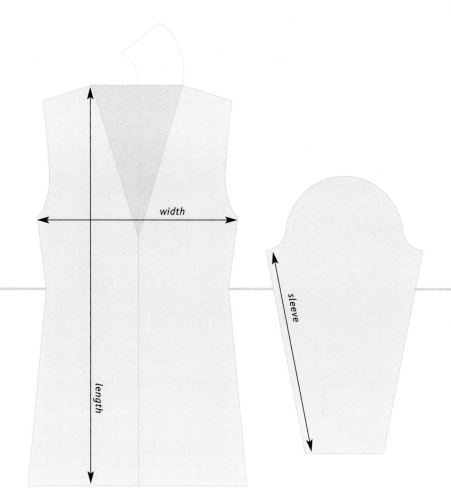

## RIGHT FRONT

With 12 mm needles cast on
30 (34:36:38:40) sts.

Cont in patt as follows:

**Foundation row:** *K3, p1; rep from * to last
10 (10:12:10:12) sts, k3 (3:5:3:5), (p1, k1)
3 times, p1.

Cont as now set, working as given for Left
Front reversing Place Pocket shapings to ***
and making buttonholes to correspond with
markers on left front as follows:

**Buttonhole row 1:** RS. Rib 3, cast off 1 st,
patt to end.

**Buttonhole row 2:** In patt, casting on 1 st
over st cast off on previous row.

### Shape neck and collar

**Row 1:** Rib 7, M1, patt 3tog, patt to end.

**Row 2:** Patt to last 8 sts, rib to end.

**Row 3:** Rib 8, M1, patt to end.

**Row 4:** Patt to last 9 sts, rib to end.

Cont as now set, working as given for Left
Front, reversing shapings.

## SLEEVES (MAKE 2)

With 12 mm needles cast on 19
(19:23:23:23) sts.

Cont in patt as given for Back, at the same
time inc 1 st at each end of the 5th and
1 (1:6:6:1) foll 4th (4th:6th:6th:4th) rows
[23 (23:37:37:27) sts], then on the 6 (6:0:0:6)
foll 6th rows. [35 (35:37:37:39) sts.]

Cont straight until Sleeve measures 46 cm
(18 in) from beg, ending with a WS row.

### Shape sleeve top

Cast off 2 (2:3:3:4) sts at beg of the next
2 rows [31 sts], then dec 1 st at each end of
the next and 3 (3:5:5:6) foll alt rows
[23 (23:19:19:17) sts], then on the next
3 (3:1:1:0) rows. Cast off rem 17 sts.

## TO MAKE UP

Join shoulders. Sew sleeve tops into armholes
then join side and sleeve seams.

Sew pocket linings in position. Sew ends of
collar together and sew in position at back of
neck. Sew on buttons.

*This simple sweater is worked in easy stocking stitch – the easiest knitted fabric to create. Knitted in pretty pastel colours, it can be worn with trousers or a skirt.*

# STRIPED SWEATER

★☆☆ VERY EASY

*This garment is very easy to knit but take care not to pull the yarn too tight when carrying the colours up the side of the work.*

## MEASUREMENTS
### To fit bust

| | | | | | |
|---|---|---|---|---|---|
| 81 | 86 | 91 | 97 | 102 | cm |
| 32 | 34 | 36 | 38 | 40 | in |

### Actual width

| | | | | | |
|---|---|---|---|---|---|
| 86 | 91 | 97 | 102 | 108 | cm |
| 34 | 36 | 38 | 40 | 42½ | in |

### Actual length

| | | | | | |
|---|---|---|---|---|---|
| 53 | 53 | 54 | 55 | 56 | cm |
| 21 | 21 | 21¼ | 21½ | 22 | in |

### Actual sleeve seam
46 cm
18 in

*In the instructions figures are given for the smallest size first; larger sizes follow in brackets. Where only one set of figures is given this applies to all sizes.*

## MATERIALS
- 4 (5:5:6:7) × 50 g balls of Rowan Cotton Glace in Stout 814 (A)
- 3 (4:4:5:6) × 50 g balls of Rowan Cotton Glace in Pier 809 (B)
- 3 (3:3:4:4) × 50 g balls of Rowan Cotton Glace in Zeal 813 (C )
- 2 (2:2:3:3) × 50 g balls of Rowan Cotton Glace in Splendour 810 (D)
- Pair each of 3 mm and 3¾ mm needles
- Stitch holders

## TENSION
22 sts and 30 rows to 10 cm (4 in) measured over stocking stitch using 3¾ mm needles.

## ABBREVIATIONS
*See page 10.*

## STRIPED SWEATER

### Striped pattern
Work 8 rows in A, 6 rows in B, 4 rows in C, 2 rows in D, 4 rows in C, 6 rows in B, 8 rows in A, 2 rows in D, 2 rows in C, 2 rows in D. These 44 rows form the patt.

### BACK
With 3 mm needles and A cast on 95 (101:107:113:119) sts and knit 9 rows. Change to 3¾ mm needles. Cont in st st beg with a knit row, working Stripe Sequence patt as above throughout, at the same time dec 1 st at each end of the 5th and 4 foll 5th rows. [85 (91:97:103:109) sts.] Work 9 rows then inc 1 st at each end of the next and 4 foll 10th rows. [95 (101:107:113:119) sts.] Work 19 rows, ending with a 6th patt row.

### Shape armholes
Cast off 6 (7:8:8:9) sts at beg of the next 2 rows [83 (87:91:97:101) sts], then dec 1 st

at each end of the next row and 4 (4:5:6:7) foll alt rows. [73 (77:79:83:85) sts.]
Work straight until armhole measures 19 (19:20:21:22) cm (7½ (7½:8:8¼:8½) in) from beg of shaping, ending with a WS row.

### Shape shoulders

Cast off 4 (5:5:5:5) sts at beg of the next 2 rows, 5 (5:5:5:6) sts on the foll 2 rows, 5 (5:5:6:6) on the foll 2 rows, 5 (5:6:6:6) on the foll 2 rows. Leave rem 35 (37:37:39:39) sts on a st holder for back neck.

### FRONT

Work as given for Back until Front measures 18 rows shorter than Back to beg of shoulder shaping, ending with a WS row.

### Shape front neck

Knit 30 (31:32:33:34) sts, turn and leave rem sts on a st holder. Work on these sts for first side.
Dec 1 st at neck edge on the next 9 rows then on the 2 foll alt rows. [19 (20:21:22:23) sts.]
Work 4 rows, ending with a WS row.

### Shape shoulder

Cast off 4 (5:5:5:5) sts at beg of the next row, 5 (5:5:5:6) sts on the foll alt row, 5 (5:5:6:6) sts on the foll alt row, work 1 row then cast off rem 5 (5:6:6:6) sts.
With RS facing, slip the centre

13 (15:15:17:17) sts on a st holder, rejoin yarn and knit to end. Complete this side to match first side, reversing shapings.

## SLEEVES (MAKE 2)

With 3 mm needles and A, cast on
44 (48:48:50:50) sts and knit 9 rows.
Change to 3¾ mm needles.
Work 130 rows to armhole, in stripe sequence and sleeve shaping as follows:
6 rows in B, 4 rows in C, 2 rows in D, 4 rows in C, 6 rows in B, 8 rows in A, 2 rows in D, 2 rows in C, 2 rows in D, (work the 44 rows of stripe patt) twice, then cont in stripe patt work 6 rows in A, at the same time shape sleeve by inc 1 st at each end of the 5th and 2 (6:14:14:18) foll 6th rows, then on the 12 (9:3:3:0) foll 8th rows.
[74 (80:84:86:88) sts.]
Cont straight until all 130 rows are completed.

### Shape sleeve top

Cast off 6 (7:8:8:9) sts at beg of the next 2 rows [62 (66:68:70:70) sts], then dec 1 st at each end of the next and 11 (10:13:13:17) foll alt rows [38 (44:40:42:34) sts], then at each end of the next 11 (13:11:11:7) rows. Cast off rem 16 (18:18:20:20) sts.

## NECKBAND

Join left shoulder. With RS facing, 3 mm needles and A, knit across 35 (37:37:39:39) sts from back neck st holder, knit up 22 sts down left front neck, knit across 13 (15:15:17:17) sts from front neck st holder, knit up 22 sts up right front neck.
[92 (96:96:100:100) sts.]
Knit 9 rows. Cast off.

## TO MAKE UP

Join right shoulder and neckband.
Sew sleeve tops into armholes then join side and sleeve seams.

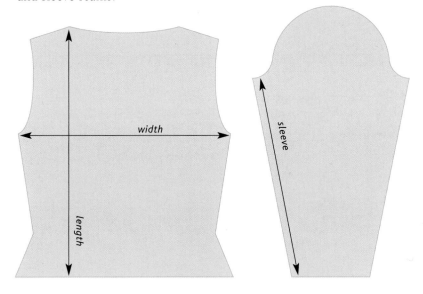

*This smart cardigan with shawl collar worked in moss st and stripes is great for wearing with a simple pair of trousers. It has a loop stitch collar and ribbon tie.*

# CARDIGAN WITH LOOP STITCH COLLAR

 ★★☆ EASY

*This cardigan is very easy to knit but the loop stitch collar takes a little more time to complete.*

## MEASUREMENTS

### To fit bust

| | | | | | | |
|---|---|---|---|---|---|---|
| 81 | 86 | 91 | 97 | 102 | 107 | cm |
| 32 | 34 | 36 | 38 | 40 | 42 | in |

### Actual width

| | | | | | | |
|---|---|---|---|---|---|---|
| 89 | 94 | 99 | 104 | 109 | 114 | cm |
| 35 | 37 | 39 | 41 | 43 | 45 | in |

### Actual length

| | | | | | | |
|---|---|---|---|---|---|---|
| 58 | 60 | 61 | 62 | 64 | 66 | cm |
| 22¾ | 23¾ | 24 | 24½ | 25¼ | 26 | in |

### Actual sleeve seam

| | | | | | | |
|---|---|---|---|---|---|---|
| 43 | 46 | 46 | 46 | 46 | 47 | cm |
| 17 | 18 | 18 | 18 | 18 | 18½ | in |

*In the instructions figures are given for the smallest size first; larger sizes follow in brackets. Where only one set of figures is given this applies to all sizes.*

## MATERIALS

- 8 (8:9:9:10:10) × 50 g balls of Rowan Summer Tweed in Storm 521 (A)
- 4 (4:4:5:5:5) × 50 g balls of Rowan Summer Tweed in Summer Berry 537 (B)
- 2 × 100 g balls of Rowan Yorkshire Tweed in Darkside 414 (C)
- Pair each of 4 mm and 5 mm needles
- 7 buttons
- Ribbon for front tie

## TENSION

16 sts and 28 rows to 10 cm (4 in) measured over moss stitch using 5 mm needles.

## ABBREVIATIONS

*See page 10.*

# CARDIGAN

## BACK

With 5 mm needles and A, cast on 71 (75:79:83:87:91) sts. Purl 2 rows.

Cont in moss st patt and stripe patt and shaping for sides as follows:

**Rows 1 to 12:** With A, *k1, p1; rep from * to last st, k1. (This row forms the moss st patt and is repeated throughout)

**Row 13:** As row 1, dec 1 st at each end of row. [69 (73:77:81:85:89) sts.]

**Row 14:** As row 1.

**Rows 15 to 18:** With C, work in moss st.

**Row 19:** With B, work as row 1, dec 1 st at each end of row. [67 (71:75:79:83:87) sts.]

**Row 20:** With B, work in moss st.

These 20 rows form the stripe patt (14 rows in A, 4 rows in C, 2 rows in B).

Cont in stripe patt throughout.

Work 4 rows in A, then cont to shape sides by dec 1 st at each end of the next and 2 foll 6th rows [61 (65:69:73:77:81) sts], then inc 1 st at each end of the foll 14th and 4 foll 10th rows. [71 (75:79:83:87:91) sts.]

Cont straight in patt until work measures 39 (41:41:41:42:43) cm (15½ (16:16:16:16½:17) in), ending with a WS row.

### Shape armholes

Cast off 4 (4:5:5:6:6) sts at beg of the next 2 rows [63 (67:69:73:75:79) sts], then dec 1 st at each end of the next and 4 (4:4:5:5:6) foll alt rows. [53 (57:59:61:63:65) sts.]
Cont straight in patt until armhole measures 19 (19:20:21:22:23) cm (7½ (7½:8:8¼:8¾:9) in), ending with a WS row.

### Shape shoulders and back neck

Cast off 5 (5:6:6:6:6) sts at beg of the next row, patt to 13 (15:15:15:16:17) sts on RH needle after cast-off, turn and leave rem sts on a st holder. Work on these sts for first side. Work 3 rows, dec 1 st at neck edge on every row and casting off 5 (6:6:6:6:7) sts for shoulder on 2nd row. Cast off rem 5 (6:6:6:7:7) sts.
With RS facing, rejoin yarn to rem sts and cast off centre 17 (17:17:19:19:19) sts, then patt to end. Complete this side to match first side, reversing shapings.

### LEFT FRONT

With 5 mm needles and A, cast on 35 (37:39: 41:43:45) sts and purl 2 rows.
Cont in moss st and stripe patt as Back. Work 12 rows then shape sides by dec 1 st at RH

edge on the next and 4 foll 6th rows [30 (32:34:36:38:40) sts], then inc 1 st at same edge on the foll 14th and 4 foll 10th rows. [35 (37:39:41:43:45) sts.] Work straight until Front matches Back to beg of armhole shaping, ending with the same patt row and at side edge.

### Shape armhole and front edge

Cast off 4 (4:5:5:6:6) sts at beg of the next row. [31 (33:34:36:37:39) sts.] Work 1 row. Dec 1 st at each end of the next row. [29 (31:32:34:35:37) sts.]
Work 8 (8:8:10:10:12) rows dec 1 st at armhole edge on the 4 (4:4:5:5:6) foll alt rows, and dec 1 st at front edge on the 2 (2:2:2:2:3) foll 4th rows. [23 (25:26:27:28:28) sts.]
Keeping armhole edge straight work 24 (24:24:28:28:12) rows dec 1 st at front edge as set on every 4th row, then work 12 (12:12:12:12:30) rows dec 1 st on every foll 6th row. [15 (17:18:18:19:20) sts.] Cont straight in patt until Front measures the same as the Back to beg of shoulder shaping, ending at armhole edge.

### Shape shoulder

Cast off 5 (5:6:6:6:6) sts at beg of the next row, 5 (6:6:6:6:7) sts on the foll alt row. Work 1 row. Cast off rem 5 (6:6:6:7:7) sts.

## RIGHT FRONT

Work as given for Left Front, reversing shapings.

## SLEEVES (MAKE 2)

With 5 mm needles and A, cast on
39 (39:41:41:43:43) sts. Purl 2 rows.
Cont in moss st and stripe patt as Back beg
with a 9th (7th:7th:7th:9th:11th) patt row.
Inc 1 st at each end of the 11th
(13th:9th:9th:9th:7th) row and 3 (7:3:3:10:1)
foll 12th (14th:10th:10th:10th:8th) row
[47 (55:49:49:65:47) sts], then on the
4 (0:6:6:0:10) foll 14th (10th:12th:12th:0th:
10th) rows. [55 (55:61:61:65:67) sts.] Cont
straight in patt until Sleeve measures
43 (46:46:46:46:47) cm
(17 (18:18:18:18:18½) in) from beg, ending
with the same patt row as Back to beg of
armhole shaping.

### Shape sleeve top

Cast off 4 (4:5:5:6:6) sts at beg of the next
2 rows. [47 (47:51:51:53:55) sts.] Dec 1 st at
each end of the next and 3 (3:4:4:3:3) foll alt
rows, then on the 4 (4:4:4:6:6) foll 4th rows,
then on the next 9 rows.
[13 (13:15:15:15:17) sts.] Cast off.

## BUTTON BAND

With 4 mm needles and A, cast on 7 sts.
**Row 1:** RS. K2, (p1, k1) twice, k1.
**Row 2:** (K1, p1) 3 times, k1.

Rep these 2 rows until button band is long
enough to fit along left front edge to beg of
front edge shaping. Cast off in rib.
Sew to front edge then mark the positions of
7 buttons, the first to come 4 rows up from
cast-on edge, the last 4 rows down from cast-
off edge and the remainder spaced evenly
between.

## BUTTONHOLE BAND

Work as given for Button band making
buttonholes to correspond with markers as
follows:
**Buttonhole row 1:** RS. Rib 3, cast off 1 st, rib
to end.
**Buttonhole row 2:** In rib, casting on over
cast-off st on previous row.

## COLLAR

Join shoulders.

### Left side

With 5 mm needles and B, cast on 5 sts.
**Row 1:** WS. Knit.
**Row 2:** K3, inc (by knitting and purling into
next st), k1, 6 sts.
**Row 3:** K1, inc in next st, k to end. [7 sts.]
**Row 4:** *K1 keeping st on LH needle bring yf,
pass yarn over left thumb to make a loop
(approximately 4 cm (1½ in), yb and knit this
st again, slipping st off the needle, yfon pass
the 2 sts just worked over this loop

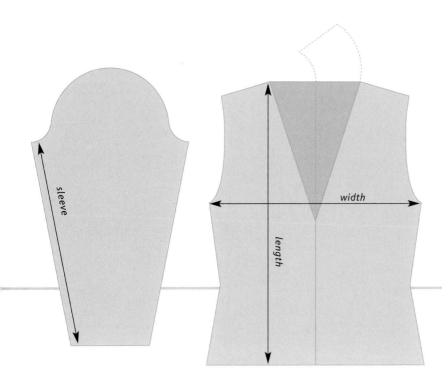

(1 loop made); rep from * to last 2 sts, inc in next st, k1, 8 sts.

**Row 5:** As row 3. [9 sts.]

**Row 6:** As row 4. [10 sts.]

Rows 3 and 4 establish loop stitch patt. Cont in loop st patt throughout, inc 1 st at the same edge on the next and 1 (1:1:3:3:3) foll alt rows [12 (12:12:14:14:14) sts], then on the 6 foll 4th rows. [18 (18:18:20:20:20) sts.]

Cont straight, keeping the k2 at the shaped edge on each loop row, until collar is of sufficient length to go along shaped edge of front to shoulder, ending with a WS row. Place a marker at shaped edge on last row.

**Next row:** Patt 16 (16:16:18:18:18), sl next st onto RH needle and take yarn to opposite side of work, between needles, sl same stitch back onto LH needle (referred to as Wrap 1), turn.

**Next row:** Knit.

**Next row:** Patt 14 (14:14:16:16:16), wrap 1, turn.

**Next row:** Knit.

**Next row:** Patt 11 (11:11:13:13:13), wrap 1, turn.

**Next row:** Knit.

**Next row:** Patt 8 (8:8:10:10:10), wrap 1, turn.

**Next row:** Knit.

**Next row:** Patt across all sts. **

Patt 11 more rows without shaping then rep from ** to ** once more.

Patt 4 more rows. Cast off loosely.

### RIGHT SIDE

With 5 mm needles and B, cast on 5 sts.

**Row 1:** WS. Knit.

**Row 2:** K1, inc, k3. [6 sts.]

**Row 3:** Knit to last 2 sts, inc, k1. [7 sts.]

**Row 4:** K1, inc, work loop patt to end. [8 sts.]

**Row 5:** As row 3. [9 sts.]

**Row 6:** As row 4. [10 sts.]

Complete as given for Left Side, reversing shapings. Cast off loosely.

### TO MAKE UP

Sew sleeve tops into armholes then join side and sleeve seams.

Join cast off edges of collar together then sew cast-on edges on collar to cast-off edges on front borders. Sew shaped edge on collar evenly around neck edges placing marker to shoulder seam.

Sew ribbon to seam under collar for approximately 3 cm (1¼ in) to secure.

*Worn together or separately this set can be worn to be smart or casual with jeans. The jacket is knitted in moss stitch to give a lovely texture and the fringed edges, which are added after the knitting is complete, add extra style. The sleeveless top is created using a finer yarn in a two-colour slip stitch pattern and also has fringing round the neck.*

# MOSS STITCH JACKET AND TOP

## HELPFUL HINTS
- Use a crochet hook or rug hook to help pull folded ends of tassels through work to speed up the process.

## MEASUREMENTS
### To fit bust

| | | | | | |
|----|----|----|----|-----|----|
| 81 | 86 | 91 | 97 | 102 | cm |
| 32 | 34 | 36 | 38 | 40 | in |

## JACKET
### Actual width

| | | | | | |
|------|------|-----|------|-----|----|
| 87.5 | 93.5 | 100 | 106 | 109 | cm |
| 34½ | 37 | 39½ | 41¾ | 43 | in |

### Actual length

| | | | | | |
|-----|------|----|------|------|----|
| 58 | 60 | 61 | 62 | 64 | cm |
| 22¾ | 23¾ | 24 | 24½ | 25¼ | in |

### Actual sleeve seam

| | | | | | |
|----|----|----|----|----|----|
| 43 | 46 | 46 | 46 | 46 | cm |
| 17 | 18 | 18 | 18 | 18 | in |

## TOP
### Actual width

| | | | | | |
|----|----|----|-----|------|----|
| 81 | 89 | 97 | 101 | 105 | cm |
| 32 | 35 | 38 | 39¾ | 41¼ | in |

### Actual length

| | | | | | |
|-----|----|-----|-----|----|----|
| 52 | 53 | 54 | 55 | 56 | cm |
| 20½ | 21 | 21¼ | 21¾ | 22 | in |

*In the instructions figures are given for the smallest size first; larger sizes follow in brackets. Where only one set of figures is given this applies to all sizes.*

## MATERIALS
### For the jacket
- 6 (6:7:7:8) × 100 g balls of Sirdar Denim Chunky 567
- Pair of 6½ mm needles
- 2 buttons

### For the top
- 2 (2:3:3:4) × 50 g balls of Sirdar Denim Tweed DK in Glacier 603 (A)
- 2 (2:3:3:4) × 50 g balls of Sirdar Denim Tweed DK in 567 (B)
- Pair each of 3¼ mm and 4 mm needles
- Stitch holders

## TENSION

### JACKET
13 sts and 22 rows to 10 cm (4 in) measured over moss stitch using 6½ mm needles.

### TOP
20 sts and 32 rows to 10 cm (4 in) measured over pattern using 4 mm needles.

## ABBREVIATIONS
*See page 10.*

★★☆ EASY

*Some knitting experience is needed to complete the jacket shapings.*

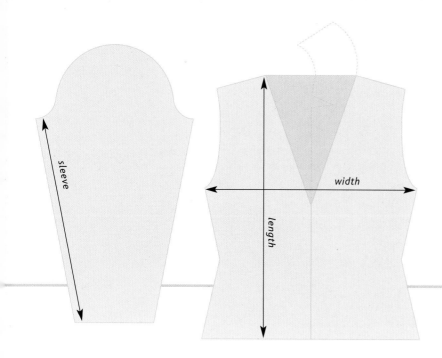

# JACKET

## BACK

With 6½ mm needles cast on 57 (61:65:69:71) sts. Cont in moss st as follows:

**Row 1:** *K1, p1; rep from * to last st, k1.
Rep this row throughout.

Shape sides by dec 1 st at each end of the 7th and 4 foll 8th rows [47 (51:55:59:61) sts], then inc 1 st at each end of the foll 8th and 4 foll 6th rows. [57 (61:65:69:71) sts.] Work straight until work measures 39 (41:41:41:42) cm (15½ (16:16:16:16½) in) from beg.

### Shape armholes

Cast off 3 (3:4:5:5) sts at beg of the next 2 rows [51 (55:57:59:61) sts], then dec 1 st at each end of the 4 foll alt rows.
[43 (47:49:51:53) sts.] Cont straight until armhole measures 19 (19:20:21:22) cm (7½ (7½:8:8¼:8¾) in) from beg of shaping.

### Shape shoulders and back neck

Cast off 4 (4:5:4:5) sts at beg of the next row, patt until there are 11 (13:13:13:13) sts on RH needle, turn and work on these sts for first side. Work 3 rows dec 1 st at neck edge on every row and casting off 4 (5:5:5:5) sts for

shoulder on 2nd row. Cast off rem 4 (5:5:5:5) sts. Rejoin yarn and cast off centre 13 (13:13:17:17) sts, patt to end. Complete this side to match first side, reversing shapings.

## LEFT FRONT

With 6½ mm needles cast on 33 (35:37:39:41) sts. Cont in moss st as Back, shaping sides by dec 1 st at RH edge on the 7th and 4 foll 8th rows [28 (30:32:34:36) sts], then inc 1 st at same edge on the foll 8th and 4 foll 6th rows. [33 (35:37:39:41) sts.] Work straight until Front measures the same as the Back to beg of armhole shaping, ending at side edge.

### Shape armhole

Cast off 3 (3:4:5:5) sts at beg of the next row [30 (32:33:34:36) sts], dec 1 st at the same edge on the 4 foll alt rows.
[26 (28:29:30:32) sts.] Cont straight until Front measures 13 rows shorter than Back to beg of shoulder shaping, ending at front edge.

### COLLAR NOTCH

Cast off 5 sts in moss st patt, turn and cast on 5 sts, patt to end.
Cont in patt until Front measures the same as the Back to beg of shoulder shaping, ending at side edge.

### Shape shoulder

Cast off 4 (4:5:4:5) sts at beg of the next row,

## FRINGING FOR JACKET

*For each tassel cut 2 lengths of yarn 7 cm (2¾ in) long, fold in half then tie in approximately 1.5 cm (¾ in) in from edge, spacing 1 cm (¼ in) apart (see page 13). Repeat all round collar edge, round outer edge on pockets, (not top pocket) and cuffs. Trim edges to neaten.*

4 (5:5:5:5) sts on the 2 foll alt rows. Cont on the rem 14 (14:14:16:17) sts for collar to centre of back neck. Cast off in patt.
Mark the positions of 2 buttons, the first 14 cm (5½ in) and the second 24 cm (9½ in) up from cast-on edge.

## RIGHT FRONT

Work as given for Left Front reversing shapings and working buttonholes at RH edge to correspond with markers.
**Buttonhole row 1:** Patt 3, (yo) twice, k2tog, patt to end.
**Buttonhole row 2:** In patt dropping one yo from previous row.

## POCKETS (MAKE 2)

With 6½ mm needles cast on 11 sts. Cont in moss st. Work 1 row then inc 1 st at each end of the next 3 rows. [17 sts.] Cont straight until pocket measures 12 cm (4¾ in) from beg. Cast off in patt.

## SLEEVES (MAKE 2)

With 6½ mm needles cast on 31 (31:33:33:35) sts and cont in moss st as Back, at the same time inc 1 st at each end of the 9th (11th: 11th:11th:7th) row and 1 (7:7:7:1) foll 10th (11th:11th:11th:8th) rows [35 (47:49:49:39) sts] then on the 5 (0:0:0:7) foll 12th (0:0:0:10th) rows. [45 (47:49:49:53) sts.] Cont straight until sleeve measures

43 (46:46:46:46) cm (17 (18:18:18:18) in) from beg.

### Shape sleeve top

Cast off 3 (3:4:5:5) sts at beg of the next 2 rows [39 (41:41:39:43) sts], then dec 1 st at each end of the 5 (5:6:6:7) foll alt rows [29 (31:29:27:29) sts], then on the 2 foll 4th rows [25 (27:25:23:25) sts], then on the next 7 rows. Cast off rem 11 (13:11:9:11) sts in patt.

## TO MAKE UP

Join shoulders. Join collar seam then sew to back of neck. Sew sleeve tops into armholes then join side and sleeve seams.
Sew pockets centrally on fronts positioning bottom of pocket 5 cm (2 in) up from cast-on edge. Sew on buttons. Add fringing (see left).

# SLEEVELESS TOP

## BACK AND FRONT (ALIKE)

With 3¼ mm needles and A, cast on 81 (89:97:101:105) sts. Work moss st border.
**Row 1:** *K1, p1; rep from * to last st, k1.
Rep this row 5 times more.
Change to 4 mm needles and cont in patt as follows:

**Preparation rows:**
**Row 1:** WS. With A, purl.
**Row 2:** With A, knit.

**Row 3:** With A, p2, *p1 wrapping yarn twice, p3; rep from * end last rep p2.
End of preparation rows.
**Row 4:** With B, k2, *sl 1 wyib dropping extra wrap, k1, insert needle into next st 2 rows below and draw through a loop loosely, knit next st and pass the loop over the st just knitted, k1; rep from * end sl 1 wyib, k2.
**Row 5:** With B, p2, *sl 1 wyif, p3; rep from * end sl 1 wyif, p2.
**Row 6:** With B, knit.
**Row 7:** With B, p2, *p1, wrapping yarn twice, p3; rep from * end last rep p2.
**Rows 8 to 11:** With A rep rows 4 to 7.
Rep rows 4 to 11 throughout.
Cont in patt until work measures 34 cm (13½ in) from beg, ending with a WS row.

### Shape armholes

Cast off 6 (6:7:7:7) sts at beg of the next 2 rows [69 (77:83:87:91) sts], then dec 1 st at each end of the next 4 rows [61 (69:75:79:83) sts], then at each end of the 3 foll alt rows. [55 (63:69:73:77) sts.]
Cont straight until armhole measures 14 (15:16:17:18) cm (5½ (6 6¼:6¾:7) in) from beg of shaping, ending with a WS row.

### Shape neck

Patt 13, turn and leave rem sts on a st holder. Work on these sts for first side. Patt 1 row. Work 11 rows dec 1 st at neck edge on every

row. [2 sts.] Cast off.
With RS facing, slip the centre 29 (37:43:47:51) sts on a st holder, rejoin yarn to rem 13 sts and patt to end. Complete this side to match first side, reversing shapings.

### NECKBAND

Join left shoulder. With RS facing, 3¼ mm needles and A, knit up 12 sts along right back neck edge, knit across 29 (37:43:47:51) sts from back neck st holder, knit up 12 sts along left back neck, 12 sts along left front neck, knit across 29 (37:43:47:51) sts from front neck st holder, knit up 13 sts up right front neck. [107 (123:135:143:151) sts.]
Work 5 rows in moss st as welt. Cast off in moss st.

### ARMBANDS (MAKE 2)

Join right shoulder and neckband.
With right side facing, 3¼ mm needles and A, knit up 91 (97:103:107:113) sts evenly along armhole edge. Work 5 rows in moss st as welt. Cast off in moss st.

### TO MAKE UP

Join sides and armhole borders. Add fringing (see above right).

### FRINGING FOR TOP

*For each tassel cut 2 lengths of yarn A, 7 cm (2¾ in) long, fold in half and tie in along first row worked for neckband approximately 1 cm (½ in) apart (see page 13). Repeat all round neckband. Trim edges to neaten.*

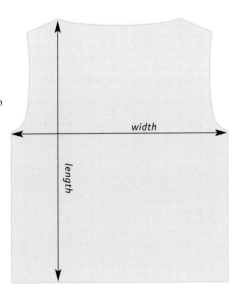

*This 'wear anywhere' garment is something special. Knitted in a fabulous yarn which changes colour magically as you knit it has ribbed raglan sleeves and a lovely cosy high collar. The main body of jacket is knitted in easy stocking stitch*

# TWO-COLOUR JACKET

★☆☆ VERY EASY

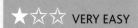 *This garment is very easy to knit but needs careful making up.*

## MEASUREMENTS
**To fit bust**

| | | | |
|---|---|---|---|
| 81–86 | 91–97 | 102–107 | cm |
| 32–34 | 36–38 | 40–42 | in |

**Actual width**

| | | | |
|---|---|---|---|
| 94 | 105 | 113 | cm |
| 37 | 41¼ | 44½ | in |

**Actual length**

| | | | |
|---|---|---|---|
| 60 | 62 | 66 | cm |
| 23¾ | 24½ | 26 | in |

**Actual sleeve seam**

| | | | |
|---|---|---|---|
| 46 | 46 | 47 | cm |
| 18 | 18 | 18½ | in |

*In the instructions figures are given for the smallest size first; larger sizes follow in brackets. Where only one set of figures is given this applies to all sizes.*

## MATERIALS
- 1 × 400 g ball of Sirdar Yo-Yo in 014
- Pair each of 3¾ mm and 4½ mm needles
- Stitch holders
- 7 buttons

## TENSION
15 sts and 24 rows to 10 cm (4 in) measured over stocking stitch using 4½ mm needles.

## ABBREVIATIONS
*See page 10.*

# JACKET

## BACK
Working from centre of ball, with 3¾ mm needles, cast on 75 (81:87) sts.

**Row 1:** RS. *K3, p3; rep from * to last 3 sts, k3.

**Row 2:** *P3, k3; rep from * to last 3 sts, p3.

Rep these 2 rows for 6 cm (2½ in) from beg, ending with a RS row.

**Next row:** Rib to end dec 4 (2:2) sts evenly across row. [71 (79:85) sts.]

Change to 4½ mm needles and cont in st st beg with a knit row.

Work 10 (10:14) rows. Work 19 rows dec 1 st at each end of the next and every foll 6th row. [63 (71:77) sts.] Work 11 rows without shaping.

Work 25 rows inc 1 st at each end of the next and every foll 8th row. [71 (79:85) sts.]

Cont without shaping until back measures 38 (38:40) cm (15 (15:15¾) in from beg, ending with a WS row.

### Shape raglans
Cast off 4 sts at beg of the next 2 rows. [63 (71:77) sts.]

Work 2 (4:4) rows dec 1 st at each end of every row. [59 (63:69) sts.]

Work 38 (40:46) rows dec 1 st at each end of the next and every foll alt row.

Cast off rem 21 (23:23) sts.

## LEFT FRONT

Working from outside of the ball, with 3¾ mm needles cast on 39 (45:51) sts.

Work 6 cm (2½ in) in rib as given for Back welt, ending with a RS row.

**Next row:** Rib 9, leave these 9 sts on a st holder for Left Front border, rib to end inc 2 sts evenly across row for 1st size only and dec 3 sts evenly across row for 3rd size only. [32 (36:39) sts.]

Change to 4½ mm needles and cont in st st. Work 10 (10:14) rows.

Work 19 rows dec 1 st at beg of the next and every foll 6th row. [28 (32:35) sts.]

Work 11 rows without shaping.

Work 25 rows inc 1 st at beg of the next and every foll 8th row. [32 (36:39) sts.]

Cont without shaping until left front measures 38 (38:40) cm (15 (15:15¾) in) from beg, ending with a WS row.

### Shape raglan

**Next row:** Cast off 4 sts, knit to end. [28 (32:35) sts.]

**Next row:** Purl.

Work 2 (4:4) rows dec 1 st at raglan edge on every row. [26 (28:31) sts.]

Work 29 (31:33) rows dec 1 st at raglan edge on the next and every foll alt row. [11 (12:14) sts.]

### Shape neck

**Next row:** Cast off 3 (4:4) sts, purl to end. [8 (8:10) sts.]

Work 2 rows dec 1 st at raglan edge on the next row, at the same time dec 1 st at neck edge on every row. [5 (5:7) sts.]

Work 5 (5:9) rows dec 1 st at raglan edge only on next and every foll alt row. [2 sts.]

**Next row:** P2tog. Fasten off.

## RIGHT FRONT

Working from outside of the ball, with 3¾ mm needles cast on 39 (45:51) sts.

Work 2 rows in rib as given for Back welt.

**Row 3:** Rib 4, cast off 2 sts, rib to end.

**Row 4:** Rib to 4 sts, cast on 2 sts, rib 4.

Cont in rib for 6 cm (2½ in), ending with a RS row.

**Next row:** Rib to last 9 sts, inc 2 sts evenly across row for 1st size only and dec 3 sts across row for 3rd size only, slip rem 9 sts onto a st holder for Right Front border. [32 (36:39) sts.]

Change to 4½ mm needles and cont in st st.

Work 10 (10:14) rows. Work 19 rows dec 1 st end of the next and every foll 6th row. [28 (32:35) sts.]

Work 11 rows without shaping.

Work 25 rows inc 1 st at end of the next and every foll 8th row. [32 (36:39) sts.]

Cont without shaping until right front measures 38 (38:40) cm (15 (15:15¾) in) from beg, ending with a RS row.

## Shape raglan

**Next row:** Cast off 4 sts, purl to end. [28 (32:35) sts.]

Work 2 (4:4) rows dec 1 st at raglan edge on every row. [26 (28:31) sts.]

Work 28 (30:32) rows dec 1 st at raglan edge on the next and every foll alt row. [12 (13:15) sts.]

## Shape neck

**Next row:** Cast off 3 (4:4) sts, knit to last 2 sts, k2tog. [8 (8:10) sts.]

**Next row:** Purl.

Work 2 rows dec 1 st at neck edge on every row, at the same time dec 1 st at raglan edge on the next row. [5 (5:7) sts.]

Work 5 (5:9) rows dec 1 st at raglan edge only on the next and every foll alt row. [2 sts.]

**Next row:** P2tog. Fasten off.

## LEFT SLEEVE

Working from the centre of the ball, with 3¾ mm needles cast on 33 sts.

Work in rib as given for Back welt for 6 cm (2½ in), ending with a WS row.

Change to 4½ mm needles and cont in rib as Back welt throughout, inc 1 st at each end of the 5th and every foll 8th (6th:2nd) row to 55 (43:39) sts, working inc sts in rib.

### 2nd and 3rd sizes only

Inc 1 st at each end of every foll (8th:6th) row to (57:63) sts, working inc sts in rib.

### All sizes

Cont without shaping until sleeve measures 46 (46:47) cm (18 (18:18½) in) from beg, ending with a WS row.

## Shape raglans

Cast off 4 sts at beg of the next 2 rows. [47 (49:55) sts.]

Work 12 (16:16) rows dec 1 st at each end of the next and every foll 4th row. [41 (41:47) sts.]

Work 28 (28:34) rows dec 1 st at each end of the next and every foll alt row.

Cast off rem 13 sts.

## RIGHT SLEEVE

Working from outside of the ball work as given for Left Sleeve.

## LEFT FRONT BAND

With RS facing and 3¾ mm needles, cast on 1 st (cast on st used to sew band to front), rib across 9 sts left on a st holder. [10 sts.]

**Row 1:** P3, k3, p3, k1.

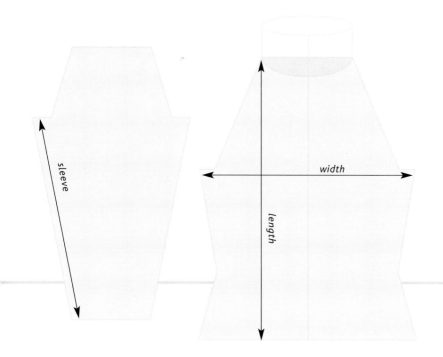

**Row 2:** P1, k3, p3, k3.

Rep these 2 rows until band is long enough to fit up front to beg of neck shaping, ending with a WS row. Break yarn and leave these sts on a st holder.

Mark the position of 6 buttons, the first to come 3 rows up from cast-on edge, the last 4 rows down from top and the remainder spaced evenly between.

### RIGHT FRONT BAND

With WS facing and 3¾ mm needles, cast on 1 st (cast-on st used to sew band to front), rib across 9 sts left on st holder. [10 sts.]

**Row 1:** K3, p3, k3, p1.

**Row 2:** K1, p3, k3, p3.

Rep these 2 rows, working buttonhole rows as given for Right Front to correspond with markers on Left Front Border until band is long enough to fit up front to beg of neck shaping, ending with a WS row. Do not break off yarn.

### NECKBAND

Join raglan seams.

With RS facing and 3¾ mm needles rib across 10 sts at top of Right Front Band as follows: k3, p3, k2, k2tog, knit up 11 (13:16) sts evenly along right side of neck, 13 sts evenly across top of left sleeve, 21 (23:23) sts evenly across back of neck, 13 sts evenly across top of right sleeve, 11 (13:16) sts evenly along left side of neck and work across 10 sts left on st holder at top of Left Front Band as follows: k2tog, k2, p3, k3. [87 (93:99) sts.]

**Next row:** Rib 9, p9 (9:10), inc in next st, (p9 (10:11), inc in next st) 5 times, p9 (10:10), rib 9. [93 (99:105) sts.]

Beg with a 1st row, work 18 rows in rib as given for Back welt.

**Next row:** Rib 4, cast off 2 sts, rib to end.

**Next row:** Rib to last 4 sts, cast on 2 sts, rib 4.

Work 3 rows in rib.

Cast off loosely in rib.

### TO MAKE UP

Join side and sleeve seams. Sew front bands in position (using cast-on sts). Sew on buttons.

*This easy-to-wear, cosy cape is knitted in two different colours and yarns which complement each other. Garter stitch ridges add extra texture.*

# TWO-COLOUR CAPE

## MEASUREMENTS

**To fit bust**

| | | |
|---|---|---|
| 81–91 | 97–107 | cm |
| 32–36 | 38–42 | in |

**Actual length (excluding fringing)**

| | | |
|---|---|---|
| 58 | 60 | cm |
| 22¾ | 23¾ | in |

**Actual width round lower edge**

| | | |
|---|---|---|
| 180 | 198 | cm |
| 71 | 78 | in |

*In the instructions figures are given for the smallest size first; larger size follows in brackets. Where only one set of figures is given this applies to both sizes.*

## MATERIALS

- 3 (4) × 100 g balls of Rowan Plaid in Red 156 (A)
- 4 (5) × 100 g balls of Rowan Chunky Print in Black 079 (B)
- Pair each of 6 mm and 8 mm needles
- Stitch holders
- 2 buttons (1 large, 1 small)

## TENSION

11½ sts and 15½ rows to 10 cm (4 in) measured over stocking stitch using 8 mm needles.

## ABBREVIATIONS

*See page 10.*

## CAPE

### RIGHT SIDE (BACK AND FRONT WORKED IN ONE PIECE)

With 6 mm needles and A, cast on 104 (114) sts. Knit 4 rows.
Change to 8 mm needles. Cont in patt as follows:
Work 8 rows in st st, beg with a knit row.
**Row 13 (dec row):** K25 (28), sl 1, k1, psso, k50 (54), k2tog, k25 (28). [102 (112) sts.]
St st 5 more rows. Knit 4 rows.
**Row 23 (dec row):** K25 (28), sl 1, k1, psso, k48 (52), k2tog, k25 (28). [100 (110) sts.]
Knit 1 row.
Work 8 rows in st st.
**Row 33 (dec row):** K25 (28), sl 1, k1, psso, k46 (50), k2tog, k25 (28). [98 (108) sts.]
St st 5 more rows.
Cont in this way, working patt – 6 rows in g st and 14 rows in st st throughout, at the same time dec in the same way as before on the next and foll 6th row. [94 (104) sts.]
Then dec on the 3 foll 4th rows, then on the 18 (20) foll alt rows. [52 (58) sts.]
Work 1 row.
**Next row:** K25 (28), sl 1, k1, psso, k25 (28). [51 (57) sts.]
**Next row:** Purl.
**Next row:** K4, *k2tog, k5(2); rep from * 6 (12) times, k2tog, k3. [44 sts.]

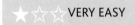

★☆☆ **VERY EASY**

*This is a really straightforward and simple pattern which can be knitted up in a short amount of time.*

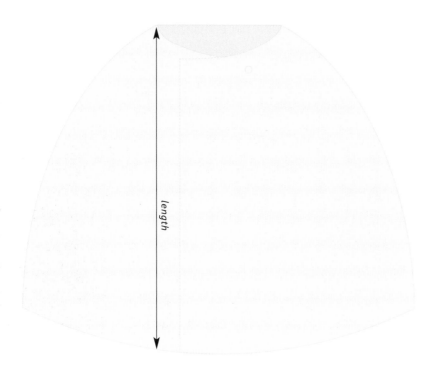

*length*

**Next row:** Purl and leave sts on a st holder.

### LEFT SIDE (BACK AND FRONT WORKED IN ONE PIECE)

With 6 mm needles and B, cast on
104 (114) sts. Knit 4 rows.
Change to 8 mm needles and cont as given for
Right Side.

### TO MAKE UP

Join centre back seam.

### NECKBAND

With RS facing and using 6 mm needles and
B, knit across 43 sts from right side, k2tog,
knit rem 43 sts from left side. [87 sts.]
Knit 1 row. Cast off.

### FRONT EDGES (MAKE 2)

With RS facing and using 6 mm needles
and B, knit up 78 sts along one front edge.
Knit 1 row. Cast off.

Sew the large button 12 cm (4¾ in) in from
left front edge and the small button at the
same distance on the wrong side on right
front. Sew a loop on each top edge to
correspond with buttons.
For each tassel cut 4 strands of yarn
approximately 25 cm (9¾ in) long, tie in
fringing evenly along lower edge (see Making
Tassels, page 13). Work fringing in A on front
worked in B, and in B on front worked in A.

ORGANIC
WHITE
£2.00

# WEEKEND

At the end of the week, it's time for relaxing and having fun and the garments in this chapter are perfect for lazy afternoons, strolls in the country and fun days out. Whether you want to just throw on a gorgeous poncho and hat knitted in a chunky soft yarn, or easy-to-wear hooded top or a knitted jacket with fashionable fur collar, there are plenty of designs in this chapter to suit every mood and style.

*An easy-to-wear, cosy ribbed and cabled cardigan with hood.
Cross stitches have been worked in a complementary colour
to add that something different.*

# HOODED CARDIGAN WITH EMBROIDERY

 EASY

 *Some knitting skill
is needed to create
the cable pattern and
cross stitch embroidery.*

 *Inserting the zip
requires neat
making up.*

## MEASUREMENTS
**To fit bust**

| | | | |
|---|---|---|---|
| 81–86 | 91–97 | 102–107 | cm |
| 32–34 | 36–38 | 40–42 | in |

**Actual width**

| | | | |
|---|---|---|---|
| 92.5 | 105 | 112.5 | cm |
| 36½ | 41¼ | 44¼ | in |

**Actual length (from shoulder)**

71 cm

28 in

**Actual sleeve seam**

| | | | |
|---|---|---|---|
| 44 | 46 | 47 | cm |
| 17¼ | 18 | 18½ | in |

*In the instructions figures are given for the
smallest size first; larger sizes follow in
brackets. Where only one set of figures is
given this applies to all sizes.*

## MATERIALS
- 11 (12:13) × 50 g balls of Rowan Cork 047
- 1 × 50 g ball of Rowan Handknit DK
  Cotton for embroidery in 313
- Pair each of 7 mm and 8 mm needles
- Cable needle
- Stitch holders
- 71 cm (28 in) open-ended zip

## TENSION
16 sts and 19 rows to 10 cm (4 in) measured
over pattern using 8 mm needles.

## ABBREVIATIONS
**C6** – slip 3 sts onto a cable needle and hold at
front, k3 then k3 from cable needle.
*See also page 10.*

## CARDIGAN

### BACK
With 7 mm needles cast on 74 (84:90) sts.
*1st and 3rd sizes*
**Row 1:** RS. K1, p1, *k6, p2; rep from * to last
8 sts, k6, p1, k1.
**Row 2:** K2, *p6, k2; rep from * to end.
*2nd size*
**Row 1:** RS. K5, *p2, k6; rep from * to last
7 sts, p2, k5.
**Row 2:** K1, p4, *k2, p6; rep from * to last
7 sts, k2, p4, k1.
*All sizes*
Work a further 10 rows as now set.
Change to 8 mm needles. Cont in patt as
follows:
*1st size*
**Row 13:** K1, p1, *C6, p2, k6, p2; rep from
* to last 8 sts, C6, p1, k1.
**Row 14:** K2, *p6, k2; rep from * to end.
*2nd size*
**Row 13:** K5, *p2, C6, p2, k6; rep from * to
last 15 sts, p2, C6, p2, k5.
**Row 14:** K1, p4, *k2, p6; rep from * to last
7 sts, k2, p4, k1.

## CROSS STITCH

*This can be worked singly (as here) or in blocks. Work a row of diagonal stitches from left to right and complete the crosses by working diagonal stitches back from right to left. Choose a nice contrast colour.*

*3rd size*

**Row 13:** K1, p1, *k6, p2, C6, p2; rep from * to last 8 sts, k6, p1, k1.

**Row 14:** K2, *p6, k2; rep from * to end.

*All sizes*

**Rows 15, 17, 19, 21 and 23:** As row 1.

**Rows 16, 18, 20, 22 and 24:** As row 2.

Rep rows 13 to 24 throughout. Cont in patt until work measures 48 (46:44) cm (19 (18:17¼) in) from beg, ending with a WS row.

### Shape raglans

Cast off 5 (6:7) sts at beg of the next 2 rows. [64 (72:76) sts.]

**Next row:** K2, k2tog, patt to the last 4 sts, k2tog-tbl, k2.

**Next row:** K1, p2, patt to last 3 sts, p2, k1.

Rep the last 2 rows 20 (22:24) times more, leave rem 22 (26:26) sts on a st holder.

### LEFT FRONT

With 7 mm needles cast on 40 (45:48) sts.

*1st and 3rd sizes*

**Row 1:** RS. K1, p1, *k6, p2; rep from * to last 6 sts, (k1, p1) twice, k2.

**Row 2:** (K1, p1) 3 times, k2, *p6, k2; rep from * to end.

*2nd size*

**Row 1:** RS. K5, p2; *k6, p2; rep from * to last 6 sts, (k1, p1) twice, k2.

**Row 2:** (K1, p1) 3 times, k2, *p6, k2; rep from * to last 5 sts, p4, k1.

*All sizes*

Work a further 10 rows as now set. **

Change to 8 mm needles. Cont in patt as follows:

*1st size*

**Row 13:** K1, p1, *C6, p2, k6, p2; rep from * to last 6 sts, (k1, p1) twice, k2.

**Row 14:** (K1, p1) 3 times, k2, *p6, k2; rep from * to end.

*2nd size*

**Row 13:** K5, p2, *C6, p2, k6, p2; rep from * to last 6 sts, (k1, p1) twice, k2.

**Row 14:** (K1, p1) 3 times, k2, *p6, k2; rep from * to last 5 sts, p4, k1.

*3rd size*

**Row 13:** K1, p1, *k6, p2, C6, p2; rep from * to last 14 sts, k6, p2, (k1, p1) twice, k2.

**Row 14:** (K1, p1) 3 times, k2, *p6, k2; rep from * to end.

*All sizes*

**Rows 15 to 24:** As Back.

Cont in patt as given for Back until work measures same as Back to beg of raglan shaping, ending with a WS row (RS on right front).

### Shape raglan

Cast off 5 (6:7) sts at beg of the next row. [35 (39:41) sts]. Work 1 row. (Omit this row on Right Front.)

**Next row:** K2, k2tog, patt to end.

**Next row:** Patt to last 3 sts, p2, k1.

Rep these 2 rows, 20 (22:24) times more.
[14 (16:16) sts.] Leave sts on a st holder.

## RIGHT FRONT

Work as given for Left Front to **.
Change to 8 mm needles. Cont in patt as
follows:

*1st size*

**Row 13:** K2, (p1, k1) twice, *p2, k6, p2, C6;
rep from * to last 2 sts, p1, k1.

*2nd size*

**Row 13:** K2, (p1, k1) twice, p2, *k6, p2, C6,
p2; rep from * to last 5 sts, k5.

*3rd size*

**Row 13:** K2, (p1, k1) twice, p2; *k6, p2, C6,
p2; rep from * to last 8 sts, k6, p1, k1.
Cont as now set. Complete as given for Left
Front, reversing shapings, ending with a WS
row. Leave sts on a st holder.

## SLEEVES (MAKE 2)

With 7 mm needles cast on 34 (38:42) sts.
**Row 1:** RS. P0 (0:2), k4 (6:6), *p2, k6; rep
from * to last 6 (8:10) sts, p2, k4 (6:6),
p0 (0:2).
**Row 2:** K0 (0, 2), p4 (6:6), k2, *p6, k2; rep
from * to last 4 (6:8) sts, p4 (6:6), k0 (0:2).
Work a further 10 rows as now set.
Change to 8 mm needles. **
**Row 13:** P0 (0:2), k4 (6:6), p2, C6, p2, k6,
p2, C6, p2, k4 (6:6), p0 (0:2).
Rep rows 13 to 24 as given for Back, at the

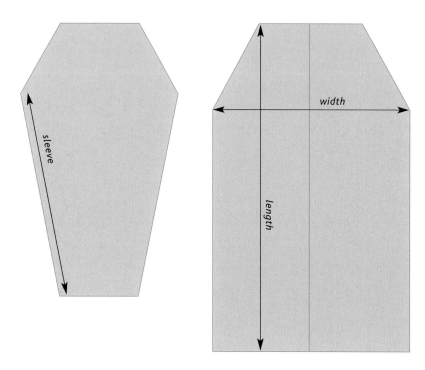

*sleeve*

*width*

*length*

same time inc 1 st at each end of the foll 4th and 0 (0:1) foll 4th rows [36 (40:46) sts], then on the 9 (10:10) foll 6th rows [54 (60:66) sts], working patt into inc sts.
Cont straight until sleeve measures 44 (46:47) cm (17¼ (18:18½) in) from beg, ending with a WS row.

### Shape raglans
Cast off 5 (6:7) sts at beg of the next 2 rows. [44 (48:52) sts.]
**Row 1:** K2, k2tog, patt to last 4 sts, k2tog-tbl, k2.
**Rows 2 and 4:** K1, p2, patt to last 3 sts, p2, k1.

**Row 3:** K3, patt to last 3 sts, k3.
Rep the last 4 rows, 4 times more [34 (38:42) sts], then dec 1 st at each end of the next and 10 (12:14) foll alt rows. [12 sts.]
Work 1 row. Leave sts on a st holder.

### HOOD
Join raglans.
With right side facing and 8 mm needles, rib 6, k8 (10:10) sts from right front st holder, knit across 12 sts from top of right sleeve, work across 22 (26:26) sts from back neck as follows:
K6 (7:7), M1, (k5 (6:6), M1) twice, k6 (7:7), knit across 12 sts from top of left sleeve, then 8 (10:10) sts from left front, rib rem 6 sts as set. [77 (85:85) sts.]
Cont in st st beg with a purl row, keeping the 6 rib sts at each end on every row, until hood measures 35 cm (13¾ in) from beg, ending with a WS row. Cast off.

### TO MAKE UP
Join hood seam. Join side and sleeve seams. Sew in zip. Make a tassel using 6 strands of yarn approximately 25 cm (10 in) long (see Making Tassels, page 13). Fold in half, wind yarn 1.5 cm (½ in) down from folded end and secure, thread yarn through loop formed and attach to point on back hood.
Work embroidered cross stitches on each rib between cables (see page 58).

*Knitted with big yarn and big needles using stocking stitch, this tweedy jacket with funky fur collar could be worn anywhere.*

# JACKET WITH FUNKY COLLAR

## MEASUREMENTS

**To fit bust**

| | | | |
|---|---|---|---|
| 81–86 | 91–97 | 102–107 | cm |
| 32–34 | 36–38 | 40–42 | in |

**Actual width**

| | | | |
|---|---|---|---|
| 100 | 110 | 120 | cm |
| 39½ | 43½ | 47¼ | in |

**Actual length**

| | | | |
|---|---|---|---|
| 57 | 59 | 61 | cm |
| 22½ | 23¼ | 24 | in |

**Actual sleeve seam**

46 cm

18 in

*In the instructions figures are given for the smallest size first; larger sizes follow in brackets. Where only one set of figures is given this applies to all sizes.*

## MATERIALS

- 9 (10:11) × 100 g balls of Sirdar Bigga in 674 (A)
- 2 (3:3) × 50 g balls of Sirdar New Fizz in 0802 (B)
- Pair each of 12 mm and 15 mm needles
- Stitch holder
- 7 buttons

## TENSION

6 sts and 9 rows to 10 cm (4 in) measured over stocking stitch using 15 mm needles.

## ABBREVIATIONS

*See page 10.*

# JACKET

## BACK

With 12 mm needles and A, cast on 29 (33:35) sts.

**Row 1:** RS. *K1, p1; rep from * to last st, k1.

**Row 2:** *P1, k1; rep from * to last st, p1.

These 2 rows form the rib. Work 2 more rows in rib inc 1 (0:1) st in centre of last row. [30 (33:36) sts.]

Change to 15 mm needles. Cont in st st, beg with a knit row.

Work 4 rows.

**Dec row:** K1, k2tog, knit to last 3 sts, sl 1, k1, psso, k1.

Work 3 rows then work the dec row once more. [26 (29:32) sts.]

Work 7 rows straight.

**Inc row:** K1, M1, knit to last st, M1, k1. [28 (31:34) sts.]

Rep the last 8 rows once more. [30 (33:36) sts.]

Cont straight as now set until work measures 34 cm (13½ in) from beg, ending with a WS row.

## Shape armholes

Cast off 2 (3:4) sts at beg of the next 2 rows [26 (27:28) sts], then dec 1 st at both ends of

 **VERY EASY**

*This garment is easy to knit but requires some care when picking up the stitches on each front edge.*

*When positioning buttons
on a cardigan, bear in
mind that the most
important buttons are the
ones at the neck, bust and
just above the hem. Place
these first and distribute
the remaining buttons
evenly along the opening.*

the next and foll alt row. [22 (23:24) sts.]
Cont straight in st st until armhole measures
23 (25:27) cm (9 (9¾:10¾) in), ending with a
WS row.

## Shape shoulders and back neck

Cast off 2 sts at beg of the next row, knit until
there are 5 sts on RH needle, turn and leave
rem sts on a st holder. Work on these sts for
first side. Cast off 2 sts at neck edge, cast off
rem 3 sts.
With RS facing, cast off the centre
8 (9:10) sts, k to end. Complete this side to
match the first side, reversing shapings.

## LEFT FRONT

With 12 mm needles and A, cast on 11
(13:13) sts and work 4 rows in rib as given for
Back welt inc 1 (0:1) st in centre on last row.
[12 (13:14) sts.]
Change to 15 mm needles. Cont in st st, beg
with a knit row.
Work 4 rows.
**Row 5 (dec):** K1, k2tog, k to end.
Dec 1 st at RH edge on the foll 4th row.
[10 (11:12) sts.]
Work 7 rows straight.
**Next row:** K1, M1, knit to end.
Rep the last 8 rows once more. [12 (13:14) sts.]
Work straight as set until Front measures the
same as the Back to beg of the armhole
shaping, ending with a WS row.

## Shape armhole

Cast off 2 (3:4) sts at beg of the next row.
[10 sts.] Work 1 row.
Dec 1 st at armhole edge on the next and foll
alt row. [8 sts.]
Cont straight until Front measures 5 rows
shorter than Back to beg of right shoulder
shaping, ending with a RS row.

## Shape neck

Cast off 1 st at beg of the next row, then dec
1 st at neck edge on the next 2 rows. [5 sts.]
Work 2 rows, ending at armhole edge.

## Shape shoulder

Cast off 2 sts at beg of the next row. Work
1 row. Cast off rem 3 sts.
Mark the positions of 7 buttons, the first
2 rows up from cast-on edge and the last
2 rows down from the cast-off neck edge and
the remainder spaced evenly between.

## RIGHT FRONT

With 12 mm needles and A, cast on 21
(23:25) sts and work 4 rows in rib as given for
Back welt inc 1 st in centre on last row.
[22 (24:26) sts.]
Change to 15 mm needles. Cont in st st, beg
with a knit row. Work 4 rows.
**Row 5 (dec):** Knit to last 3 sts, sl 1, k1, psso, k1.
Dec 1 st at LH edge on the foll 4th row.
[20 (22:24) sts.]

Work 7 rows.

**Next row:** Knit to last st, M1, k1.

Rep the last 8 rows once more.

[22 (24:26) sts.]

Cont until work measures the same as the Back to beg of armhole shaping, ending with a RS row.

### Shape armhole

Cast off 2 (3:4) sts at beg of the next row. [20 (21:22) sts.] Dec 1 st at armhole edge on the next and foll alt row.

[18 (19:20) sts.]

Cont straight until work measures 5 rows shorter than Back to left shoulder, ending at front edge.

### Shape neck

Cast off 11 (12:13) sts at beg of the next row [7 sts], then dec 1 st at neck edge on the next 2 rows. [5 sts.]

Work 2 rows, ending at armhole edge.

### Shape shoulder

Cast off 2 sts at beg of the next row. Work 1 row. Cast off rem 3 sts.

### SLEEVES (MAKE 2)

With 12 mm needles and A, cast on 13 (15:17) sts and work 4 rows in rib as given for Back welt inc 1 st in centre on last row. [14 (16:18) sts.]

Change to 15 mm needles. Cont in st st, beg with a knit row. Work 4 rows then inc 1 st at each end of the next and 4 foll 6th rows. [24 (26:28) sts.] Cont straight until sleeve measures 46 cm (18 in) from beg, ending with a WS row.

## Shape sleeve top
Cast off 2 (3:4) sts at beg of the next 2 rows. [20 sts.]
**Next row:** K2tog, k to last 2 sts, sl 1, k1, psso. [18 sts.]
Dec 1 st at each end of the 0 (1:1) foll 4th rows. [18 (16:16) sts.] Dec 1 st at each end of the 3 (2:2) foll alt rows. [12 sts.]
**Next row:** WS. P2tog-tbl, purl to last 2 sts, p2tog. [10 sts.]
Work 3 more rows dec 1 st at each end of every row. [4 sts.] Cast off.

## FRONT BANDS (MAKE 2)
With RS facing and using 12 mm needles and A, knit up 35 (36:37) sts along one front edge. Knit 1 row. Cast off.

## COLLAR
Note: The purl side is the right side of the work. Join shoulders.
With 15 mm needles and B, cast on 106 (112:118) sts. Cont in st st until collar measures 21 cm (8¼ in) from beg. Cast off loosely.

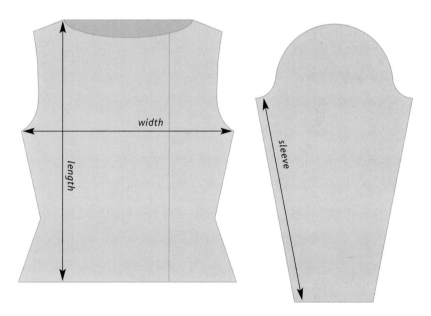

## TO MAKE UP
Sew cast-on edge of collar to neck edge. Sew sleeve tops into armholes then join side and sleeve seams. Sew on buttons. Use natural holes in fabric for buttons to fasten.

*This glorious patchwork pattern is slightly more challenging to complete but your efforts will be worthwhile. The stocking stitch coat with ribbed collar and added tassels is a real show stopper.*

# PATCHWORK COAT

★★★ MEDIUM

 *The stitch used in this garment (stocking stitch) is very simple to work.*

 *This project is slightly more challenging because of the number of colour changes.*

## HELPFUL HINTS

- When working with different coloured yarns, use the Intarsia technique. Twist the new colour round the colour just used to link the colours together and avoid holes. Do not break off and join in except where absolutely necessary.

## MEASUREMENTS

### To fit bust

| | | |
|---|---|---|
| 81–91 | 97–107 | cm |
| 32–36 | 38–42 | in |

### Actual width

| | | |
|---|---|---|
| 114 | 128 | cm |
| 45 | 50½ | in |

### Actual length

| | | |
|---|---|---|
| 94 | 99 | cm |
| 37 | 39 | in |

### Actual sleeve seam (with cuff turned back)

| | | |
|---|---|---|
| 41 | 42 | cm |
| 16 | 16½ | in |

*In the instructions figures are given for the smallest size first; larger size follows in brackets. Where only one set of figures is given this applies to both sizes.*

## MATERIALS

- 4 (5) × 100 g balls of Sirdar Denim Chunky in Denim Blue Marl 516 (A)
- 3 (4) × 100 g balls of Sirdar Denim Chunky in Ivory Cream 508 (B)
- 2 (3) × 100 g balls of Sirdar Denim Chunky in Denim Blue 502 (C)
- 2 (3) × 100 g balls of Sirdar Denim Chunky in Camel 613 (D)
- Pair each of 5½ mm and 6½ mm needles
- 4 toggles

## TENSION

14 sts and 19 rows to 10 cm (4 in) measured over stocking stitch using 6½ mm needles.

## ABBREVIATIONS

*See page 10.*

# COAT

## BACK

With 5½ mm needles and A, cast on 78 (90) sts.

**Row 1:** RS. *K2, p2; rep from * to last 2 sts, k2.

**Row 2:** *P2, k2; rep from * to last 2 sts, p2.
These 2 rows form the 2x2 rib. Work 8 more rows in rib inc 2 (0) sts evenly on last row. [80 (90) sts.]
Change to 6½ mm needles. Cont in patt as follows:

**Row 1:** RS. K8 (9) A, k16 (18) B, k16 (18) C, k16 (18) D, k16 (18) B, k8 (9) A.

**Row 2:** P8 (9) A, p16 (18) B, p16 (18) D, p16 (18) C, p16 (18) B, p8 (9) A.

Rep these 2 rows 16 (17) times more.
[34 (36) patt rows.]
**Row 35 (37):** K8 (9) C, k16 (18) D, k16 (18)
B, k16 (18) A, k16 (18) D, k8 (9) C.
**Row 36 (38):** P8 (9) C, p16 (18) D, p16 (18)
A, p16 (18) B, p16 (18) D, p8 (9) C.
Rep these 2 rows 16 (17) times more.
[34 (36) patt rows.]
Rep rows 1 to 68 (72), then rows 1 to 34 (36)
once more. Cast off.

## LEFT FRONT

With 5½ mm needles and A, cast on
38 (46) sts and work 10 rows in 2x2 rib as
given for Back welt inc 2 (dec 1) st evenly on
last row. [40 (45) sts.]
Change to 6½ mm needles. Cont in patt as
follows:
**Row 1:** RS. K8 (9) A, k16 (18) B, k16 (18) C.
Work a further 33 (35) rows as set.
**Row 35 (37):** K8 (9) C, k16 (18) D,
k16 (18) B.
Work a further 33 (35) rows as set.
Rep rows 1 to 34 (36) then rows 35 (37) to
52 (54) once, ending with a WS row.
[120 (126) rows.]

## Shape front slope

**Next row:** Work in patt to the last 2 sts, sl 1,
k1, psso. Place a marker at end of row.
Patt 3 rows. Rep these 4 rows 6 (7) times
more, omitting markers. [33 (37) sts.]

**Next row:** Patt to the last 2 sts, sl 1, k1, psso.
Patt 5 rows. Rep these 6 rows once more.
**Next row:** Patt to last 2 sts, sl 1, k1, psso.
[30 (34) sts.]
Work 9 rows straight. Cast off.

## RIGHT FRONT

With 5½ mm needles and A, cast on
38 (46) sts and work 10 rows in 2x2 rib as
given for Back welt inc 2 (dec 1) st evenly on
last row. [40 (45) sts.]
Change to 6½ mm needles. Cont in patt as
follows:
**Row 1:** Right side. K16 (18) D, k16 (18) B,
k8 (9) A.
Work a further 33 (35) rows as set.
**Row 35 (37):** K16 (18) A, k16 (18) D,
k8 (9) C.
Work a further 33 (35) rows as set.
Rep rows 1 to 34 (36) then rows 35 (37) to
52 (54) once, ending with a WS row.
[120 (126) rows.]

## Shape front slope

**Next row:** Place a marker. K2tog, patt to end.
Complete as given for Left Front, reversing
shapings.

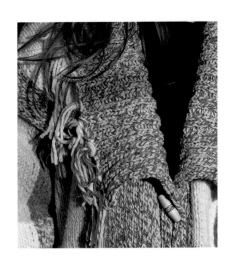

## RIGHT SLEEVE

With 5½ mm needles and A, cast on
58 (62) sts and work 18 cm (7 in) in 2x2 rib as
given for Back welt ending with a WS row.

**Dec row:** Rib 1 (5), *rib 2tog, rib 4 (5); rep
from * 9 (7) times, rib 2tog, rib 1 (6).
[48 (54) sts.]

Change to 6½ mm needles. *** Cont in patt
as follows:

**Row 1:** RS. K8 (9) A, k16 (18) B, k16 (18) C,
k8 (9) D.

Cont as now set inc 1 st at each end of the
2 foll 4th rows [52 (58) sts], then on the 4 foll
6th rows. [60 (66) sts.] Work 1 (3) rows.
[34 (36) rows.]

**Row 35 (37):** K14 (15) C, k16 (18) D, k16
(18) B, k14 (15) A.

Cont as now set inc 1 st at each end of the foll
5th (3rd) and 3 foll 6th rows. [68 (74) sts.]
Work 3 (5) rows straight.

### Shape top

Work 7 rows dec 1 st at each end of every row.
[54 (60) sts.] Cast off.

## LEFT SLEEVE

Work as given for Right Sleeve to ***.
Cont in patt as follows:

**Row 1:** RS. K8 (9) D, k16 (18) C, k16 (18) B,
k8 (9) A.

Cont as now set inc 1 st at each end of the
2 foll 4th rows [52 (58) sts], then on the 4 foll
6th rows. [60 (66) sts.]
Work 1 (3) rows. [34 (36) rows.]

**Row 35 (37):** K14 (15) A, k16 (18) B, k16
(18) D, k14 (15) C.

Complete as given for Right Sleeve.

## BUTTON BAND AND COLLAR

Join shoulders.

With 5½ mm needles and A, cast on 10 sts
and work in 2x2 rib as given for Back welt
until piece is long enough, when slightly
stretched, to fit up Left Front to marker **,
ending with a WS row. Mark end of last row
with a coloured thread.

### Shape collar

**Next row:** Cast on 62 (66) sts, *p2, k2; rep
from * to end. Rep this row. [72 (76) sts.]
Cont in rib as set until Collar measures 8 cm
(3 in) from cast-on edge.

Change to 6½ mm needles and work a further
6 cm (2½ in) in rib as set. Cast off in rib.
Matching markers, sew Band to Left Front
then sew Collar neatly in place to centre back
of neck.

Mark the positions of 4 toggles on Band, the
first to come 28 (30.5) cm (11 (11¼ in) up
from cast-on edge and the last 2 cm (¾ in)
down from marker and the remainder spaced
evenly between.

## BUTTONHOLE BAND AND COLLAR

Work as given for Button Band to **, ending with a RS row, marking end of last row with a coloured thread and working buttonholes to correspond with markers as follows:

**Buttonhole row 1:** RS. Rib 4, cast off next 2 sts, rib to end.

**Buttonhole row 2:** Rib, casting on over sts cast off on previous row.

Complete to match Button Band and Collar, working rib across all sts, *k2, p2; rep from * to end.

Matching markers, sew Band to Right Front then sew Collar neatly in place to centre back of neck. Join centre back seam of Collar.

## TO MAKE UP

Mark depth of armhole 24 (26.5) cm (9½ (10½ in) from shoulder seam. Sew sleeve tops between markers then join side and sleeve seams, reversing seam on the last 9 cm (3½ in) for cuff. Sew on toggles.

For each tassel cut one 25 cm (9¾ in) length of each of the four colours.

Tie in tassels evenly spaced along collar edge (see Making Tassels, page 13).

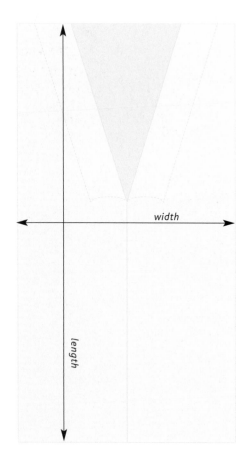

*This gorgeous poncho is so cosy. Knitted on the largest needles, the garment grows very quickly as you knit so although it is a large piece, it won't take you hours to complete. The tassels and large polo collar add a finishing touch – you won't want to take it off.*

# PONCHO AND HAT WITH EARFLAPS

## HELPFUL HINTS
- The yarn alternates between thin, smooth threads and soft, furry nubs. While textured yarns can be difficult to knit, this one is easily knitted because the needle catches the smooth parts of the yarn neatly.
- You'll find that this garment grows quickly. Every time you work a row, you will be a centimetre closer to finishing!

## MEASUREMENTS
**To fit bust**
86–102 cm
34–40 in
**Actual length (without collar and fringes)**
64 cm
25 in

## MATERIALS

**For the poncho**
- 18 × 50 g balls of Rowan Big Wool Tuft in Frosty 055
- Pair each of 15 mm and 20 mm needles.

**For the hat with earflaps**
- 2 × 50 g balls of Rowan Big Wool Tuft in Frosty 055
- Pair of 20 mm needles

## TENSION
5½ sts and 7 rows to 10 cm (4 in) measured over stocking stitch using 20 mm needles.

## ABBREVIATIONS
*See page 10.*

# PONCHO

## BACK AND FRONT
With 15 mm needles cast on 79 sts. Purl 4 rows.
Change to 20 mm needles. Cont in st st beg with a knit row. Work 2 rows. Place a marker on the centre (40th) st.

## Shape body
**Row 1:** K1, k2tog, knit to within 2 sts of marked st, k2tog-tbl, k2tog, knit to last 3 sts, k2tog-tbl, k1.
**Row 2:** Purl.
**Row 3:** Knit to within 2 sts of marked st, k2tog-tbl, k1, k2tog, knit to end.
**Row 4:** Purl.
Rep the last 4 rows, 9 times more. [19 sts.]
Cast off.

## COLLAR
With RS facing and 15 mm needles, knit up 16 sts from front, then 16 sts from back. [32 sts.]

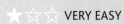 VERY EASY

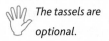 *Although this garment uses a textured yarn, it is still very easy to knit and will grow quickly.*

*With no sleeves to make and very simple shaping, this is one of the simplest types of garment to create.*

*The tassels are optional.*

## VARIATION: HAT WITH BRIM

To make this hat you will need 2 × 50 g balls of Rowan Big Wool Tuft in Frosty 055. With 20 mm needles cast on 28 sts. Cont in st st beg with a knit row until the hat measures 20 cm (8 in) from beg, ending with a WS row.

### Shape crown

Work as for hat with earflaps.

### TO MAKE UP

Break yarn and thread through sts, pull up tightly and secure. Sew back seam, reversing seam on hat on the last 6 cm (2½ in) for brim. Press as instructions given on ball band.

---

Work in rev st st, beg with a purl row, for 10 cm (4 in). Change to 20 mm needles. Cont in rev st st until collar measures 20 cm (8 in) from beg. Knit 4 rows. Cast off loosely.

### TO MAKE UP

Press as instructions given on ball band. Join back and front seam and collar seam, reversing collar seam for turn-back. Along lower edge, tie in fringes that are about 12 cm (4¾ in) long, made with double yarn and spaced 3 sts apart.

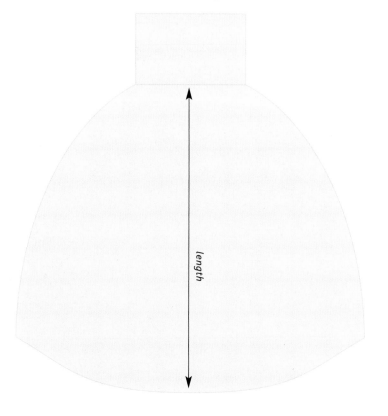

*length*

## HAT WITH EARFLAPS

### RIGHT EARFLAP

With 20 mm needles cast on 5 sts.
Cont in st st.
**Row 1:** Knit.
**Row 2:** Purl inc 1 st at both ends of row.
**Row 3:** Knit. **.
**Row 4:** Purl inc 1 st at end of row only. [8 sts.]
Work 2 rows and leave sts on a st holder.

### LEFT EARFLAP

Work as given for Right Earflap side to **.
**Row 4:** Purl inc 1 st at beg of row only. [8 sts.]

### BODY OF HAT

With 20 mm needles cast on 2 sts, knit across 8 sts from one ear flap, cast on 8 sts, knit across 8 sts from second ear flap, cast on 2 sts. [28 sts.]
Cont in st st beg with a purl row until main body of hat measures 15 cm (6 in) from cast-on edge, ending with a WS row.

### Shape crown

**Row 1:** K1, (k2tog, k2) 6 times, k2tog, k1. [21 sts.]
**Row 2:** Purl.
**Row 3:** K1, (k2tog, k1) 6 times, k2tog. [14 sts.]
**Row 4:** Purl.
**Row 5:** (K2tog) 7 times. [7 sts.]

*Watch the heads turn with envy when you wear this unusual pointed sweater with centre cable and fringing. If you prefer, you can add beads to the fringes – just make sure you choose ones with large holes.*

# SWEATER WITH FRINGING

 ★★☆ EASY

*Some knitting skill is needed to create the cable design.*

*The fringing requires neat and careful making up.*

## MEASUREMENTS
**To fit bust**

| | | | |
|---|---|---|---|
| 81–86 | 91–97 | 102–107 | cm |
| 32–34 | 36–38 | 40–42 | in |

**Actual width**

| | | | |
|---|---|---|---|
| 96 | 106 | 116 | cm |
| 37¾ | 41¾ | 45¾ | in |

**Actual length (excluding fringing)**

| | | | |
|---|---|---|---|
| 49 | 51 | 53 | cm |
| 19¼ | 20 | 20¾ | in |

**Actual sleeve seam**

| | | | |
|---|---|---|---|
| 43 | 46 | 46 | cm |
| 17 | 18 | 18 | in |

*In the instructions figures are given for the smallest size first; larger sizes follow in brackets. Where only one set of figures is given this applies to all sizes.*

## MATERIALS
- 7 (8:9) × 100 g balls of Rowan Chunky Print in Girly Pink 077
- Pair each of 7 mm and 8 mm needles
- Stitch holders
- Cable needle

## TENSION
12 sts and 15½ rows to 10 cm (4 in) measured over stocking stitch using 8 mm needles.

## ABBREVIATIONS
**C6** – slip next 3 sts to cable needle and hold at back, k3 then k3 from cable needle
*See also page 10.*

## SWEATER

**Cable pattern – worked over 6 sts**
**Rows 1 and 3:** RS. Knit.
**Rows 2 and 4:** Purl.
**Row 5:** C6.
**Rows 6 and 8:** Purl.
**Row 7:** Knit.
These 8 rows form the patt and are repeated throughout.

### BACK
With 8 mm needles cast on 6 sts.
**Row 1:** RS. Knit.
**Row 2:** Purl.
**Row 3:** Cast on 3 sts, k1, p2 on these 3 sts, k6.
**Row 4:** Cast on 3 sts, p1, k2 on these 3 sts, p6, k2, p1.
**Row 5:** Cast on 2 sts, k3, p2, C6, p2, k1.
**Row 6:** Cast on 2 sts, p3, k2, p6, k2, p3. [16 sts.]
Working the 8 row cable patt on the centre 6 sts, inc at sides as follows:
*Cast on 3 sts at beg of the next 2 rows then 2 sts on the foll 2 rows, working inc sts in st st * rep from * to * 2 (3:3) more times.
[46 (56:56) sts.]

*1st size*
Cast on 3 sts at beg of the next 4 rows. [58 sts.]
*2nd size*
Cast on 4 sts at beg of the next 2 rows. [64 sts.]
*3rd size*
Cast on 3 sts at beg of the next 2 rows, cast on 4 sts at beg of the next 2 rows. [70 sts.]
*All sizes*
Cont as now set until side seam measures 30 cm (11¾ in) from end of shaping, ending with a WS row.

## Shape armholes

Cast off 3 (4:5) sts at beg of the next 2 rows [52 (56:60) sts], then dec 1 st at each end of the next 3 rows [46 (50:54) sts], then on the 3 (3:4) alt rows. [40 (44:46) sts.] Cont straight until armhole measures 19 (21:23) cm (7½ (8¼:9) in) from beg of shaping, ending with a WS row.

## Shape shoulders and back neck

Cast off 4 (5:5) sts at beg of the next row, knit until there are 8 sts on RH needle, turn and leave rem sts on a st holder. Work on these sts for first side.
Cast off 3 sts at neck edge on next row. Cast off rem 5 sts.
With RS facing, slip the centre 16 (18:20) sts on a st holder, rejoin yarn at neck edge and knit to end. Complete this side to match first side, reversing shapings.

## FRONT

Work as given for Back until Front measures 16 rows shorter than Back to beg of shoulder shaping, ending with a WS row.

## Shape neck

**Next row:** Knit until there are 14 (15:15) sts on RH needle, turn and leave rem sts on a st holder. Work on these sts for first side.
Work 10 rows dec 1 st at neck edge on every alt row. [9 (10:10) sts.]
Work 5 rows, ending with a WS row.

## Shape shoulder

Cast off 4 (5:5) sts at beg of the next row.
Work 1 row. Cast off rem 5 sts.
Slip the centre 12 (14:16) sts on a st holder. Rejoin yarn and knit to end. Complete this side to match first side, reversing shapings.

## SLEEVES (MAKE 2)

With 7 mm needles cast on 27 (29:31) sts and knit 4 rows inc 1 st in centre of last row. [28 (30:32) sts.]
Change to 8 mm needles. Cont in st st, beg with a knit row. Work 18 rows.
Inc 1 st at each end of the next and 2 (3:3) foll 12th (10th:10th) rows. [34 (38:40) sts.]
Cont straight until Sleeve measures 43 (46:46) cm (17 (18:18) in) from beg, ending with a WS row.

### Shape sleeve top

Cast off 3 (4:4) sts at beg of the next 2 rows
[28 (30:32) sts], then dec 1 st at each end of
the next and 6 (7:8) foll alt rows [14 sts], then
on the next 3 rows. [8 sts.] Cast off.

### LOWER EDGE (MAKE 2)

With 7 mm needles cast on 8 sts.
**Row 1:** K8.
**Row 2:** P4, k3, p1.
Rep these 2 rows until piece fits along lower
edge (do not stretch around point) ending
with a 2nd row.
**Final row:** Cast off 4 sts, draw yarn through
rem st on right hand needle, slip rem 3 sts off
needle and unravel them all the way down to
make fringe loops.

### COLLAR

Join left shoulder.
With RS facing and 7 mm needles, knit
up 2 sts from right back neck, knit across
16 (18:20) sts from back neck st holder, knit
up 2 sts from left back neck, 15 sts down left
front neck, knit across 12 (14:16) sts from
front neck st holder, knit up 15 sts up right
front neck. [62 (66:70) sts.]
Cont in g st (every row knit) until collar
measures 14 cm (5½ in). Change to 8 mm
needles and cont in g st until collar measures
28 cm (11 in) from beg. Cast off loosely.

### TO MAKE UP

Join right shoulder and collar reversing seam
on the last 15 cm (6 in). Sew sleeve tops into
armholes then join side and sleeve seams.
Sew edging to lower edges.

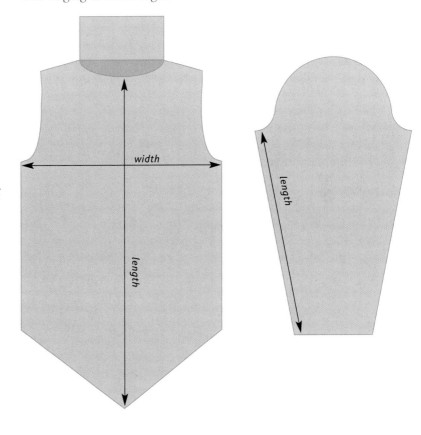

*Knit in an evening! This stocking stitch wrap is knitted in a vibrant yarn for an eye-catching look.*

# THROW-OVER WRAP

★ ☆ ☆ VERY EASY

 *This project couldn't be simpler. The chunky yarn and large needles mean that it can be completed in a very short amount of time.*

## MEASUREMENTS
Actual width
127 cm
50 in
Actual length (excluding fringing)
78 cm
30¾ in

## MATERIALS
- 18 × 100 g balls of Rowan Biggy in 246
- Pair each of 15 mm and 20 mm needles

## TENSION
5½ sts and 7 rows to 10 cm (4 in) measured over stocking stitch using 20 mm needles.

## ABBREVIATIONS
*See page 10.*

## WRAP

### LEFT SIDE
With 15 mm needles cast on 32 sts.
Knit 5 rows for hem.
Change to 20 mm needles.
**Next row:** WS. K2, purl to last 2 sts, k2.
**Next row:** Knit.
These 2 rows form the patt and are repeated throughout. **
Cont in patt until work measures 78 cm (30¾ in) from beg, ending with a RS row.

**Next row:** Cast on 3 sts for back neck, knit across these 3 sts, k2 then purl to last 2 sts, k2. [35 sts.]
**Next row:** Knit.
**Next row:** Purl to last 2 sts, k2.
Rep the last 2 rows until back measures same as front to top of hem, ending with a RS row.
Change to 15 mm needles.
Knit 3 rows. Cast off knitwise.

### RIGHT SIDE
Work as given for Left Side to **.
Cont in patt until work measures 78 cm (30¾ in) from beg, ending with a WS row.
**Next row:** Cast on 3 sts for back neck, purl across these 3 sts, purl 2, then knit to end. [35 sts.]
**Next row:** K2, purl to end.
**Next row:** Knit.
Rep the last 2 rows until back measures same as front to top of hem, ending with a RS row.
Change to 15 mm needles.
Knit 3 rows. Cast off knitwise.

### TO MAKE UP
Join centre back seam neatly.
For each tassel cut 3 lengths of yarn each 25 cm (9¾ in) long and tie in evenly along lower edges (see Making Tassels, page 13).

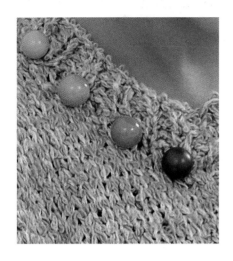

# CASUAL

Casual elegance for everyday dressing, what could be easier to wear? These knitted cardigans, sweaters and tops are gorgeously cosy yet big on style, with simple stitch patterns and luxurious yarns. From the sweater with frilled edges in a textured cotton yarn to the striped sleeveless top worked in a chenille yarn with its velvety pile, these are all wonderfully easy to wear. All the patterns are easy to knit while some are ideal for the complete beginner – there is something here to suit everyone.

*Dress up any garment with this cardigan worked in stocking stitch with a striped border pattern. The zigzag effect is created simply by increasing and decreasing at regular intervals. The cardigan is tied round the waist with ribbon and has coordinating ribbon on the cuffs.*

# CARDIGAN WITH RIBBON TIES

★★☆ EASY

 *The challenging part of this project is in the zigzag design.*

## MEASUREMENTS
**To fit bust**

| | | | |
|---|---|---|---|
| 81–86 | 91–97 | 102–107 | cm |
| 32–34 | 36–38 | 40–42 | in |

**Actual width**

| | | | |
|---|---|---|---|
| 91 | 102 | 113 | cm |
| 36 | 40 | 44½ | in |

**Actual length (to lowest hem point)**

| | | | |
|---|---|---|---|
| 62 | 65 | 68 | cm |
| 24½ | 25½ | 26¾ | in |

**Actual sleeve seam (to lowest cuff point)**

| | | | |
|---|---|---|---|
| 49 | 51 | 51 | cm |
| 19¼ | 20 | 20 | in |

*In the instructions figures are given for the smallest size first; larger sizes follow in brackets. Where only one set of figures is given this applies to all sizes.*

## MATERIALS
- 10 (11:12) × 50 g balls of Rowan Wool Cotton in Poster Blue 948 (A)
- 1 × 50 g ball of Rowan Wool Cotton in Antique 900 (B)
- 1 × 50 g ball of Rowan Wool Cotton in French Navy 909 (C )
- Pair each of 3¼ mm and 4 mm needles
- Stitch holder
- Ribbon for waist and cuffs
- 9 buttons

## TENSION
22 sts and 30 rows to 10 cm (4 in) measured over stocking stitch using 4 mm needles.

## ABBREVIATIONS
*See page 10.*

# CARDIGAN

## BACK
With 4 mm needles and A, cast on 128 (146:164) sts and purl 3 rows.
Cont in patt as follows:

**Row 1:** WS. With A, purl.

**Row 2:** With A, k1, inc in next st (by knitting into front and back of st), k6, sl 1, k1, psso, k2tog, k6, *inc in each of next 2 sts, k6, sl 1, k1, psso, k2tog, k6; rep from * to last 2 sts, inc in next st, k1.

**Row 3:** With A, purl.

**Row 4:** As row 2.

Work 3 more rows in A, 4 rows in B, 2 rows in C, 2 rows in A as now set.

**Row 16 (dec row):** RS. With A, k1, inc in next st, k2, k2tog, k2, sl 1, k1, psso, (k2tog, k2) twice; *inc in each of next 2 sts, k2, k2tog, k2, sl 1, k1, psso, (k2tog, k2) twice; rep from * to last 2 sts, inc in next st, k1.
[114 (130:146) sts.]

**Row 17 and 19:** With A, purl.

**Row 18:** With A, k1, inc in next st, k5, sl 1, k1, psso, k2tog, k5, *inc in each of next 2 sts,

k5, sl 1, k1, psso, k2tog, k5; rep from * to last 2 sts, inc in next st, k1.

Work 3 more rows in A, 4 rows in B, 2 rows in C, 2 rows in A as now set.

**Row 30 (dec row):** RS. With A, k1, inc in next st, k1, k2tog, k2, sl 1, k1, psso, k2tog, k1, k2tog, k2, *inc in each of next 2 sts, k1, k2tog, k2, sl 1, k1, psso, k2tog, k1, k2tog, k2; rep from * to last 2 sts, inc in next st, k1. [100 (114:128) sts.]

**Row 31:** With A, purl.

**Row 32:** With A, k1, inc in next st, k4, sl 1, k1, psso, k2tog, k4, * inc in each of next 2 sts, k4, sl 1, k1, psso, k2tog, k4; rep from * to last 2 sts, inc in next st, k1.

Work 15 more rows in A as now set (47 patt rows have been worked).

**Eyelet and dec row:** With A, k1, (k2tog, yon) twice, [(k2tog, yon) twice, k3tog, yon] 12 (14:16) times, (k2tog, yon) 5 times, k1. [88 (100:112) sts.]

**Next row:** With A, purl.

Cont in st st and A, beg with a knit row, at the same time inc 1 st at each end of the foll 7th (7th:9th) and 5 foll 8th (9th:9th) rows [100 (112:124) sts], then cont straight until work measures 22 (23:24) cm (8½ (9:9½) in) from top of eyelet row, ending with a WS row.

## Shape armholes

Cast off 6 (7:9) sts at beg of the next 2 rows [88 (98:106) sts], then dec 1 st at each end of the next 5 (5:7) rows, then on the 0 (2:2) foll alt rows. [78 (84:88) sts.] Cont straight until armhole measures 19 (21:23) cm (7½ (8¼:9) in) from beg of shaping, ending with a WS row.

## Shape shoulders and back neck

Cast off 6 sts at beg of the next row, knit until there are 22 (24:25) sts on RH needle after cast off, turn and leave rem sts on a st holder. Work on these sts for the first side. Dec 1 st at neck edge on next row. Cast off 6 (6:7) sts for shoulder on next row and dec 1 st at neck edge. Dec 1 st at neck edge on next row. Cast off 6 (7:7) sts at shoulder on next row and dec 1 st at neck edge. Work 1 row. Cast off rem 6 (7:7) sts. With RS facing, rejoin yarn and cast off centre 22 (24:26) sts, knit to end. Complete this side to match the first side, reversing shapings.

## LEFT FRONT

With 4 mm needles and A, cast on 65 (74:83) sts and purl 3 rows.

Cont in patt as follows:

*1st and 3rd sizes*

**Row 1:** WS. With A, purl.

**Row 2:** With A, k1, inc in next st, k6, sl 1, k1, psso, k2tog, k6, *inc in each of the next 2 sts, k6, sl 1, k1, psso, k2tog, k6; rep from * to last 11 sts, inc in each of the next 2 sts, k6, sl 1, k1, psso, k1.

*2nd size*

As given for Back.

## All sizes

Cont as now set and in same stripe sequence as Back.

### 1st and 3rd sizes

**Row 16 (dec row):** Work in same way as given for Back to the last 11 sts, inc in each of next 2 sts, k2, k2tog, k2, sl 1, k1, psso, k1. [58 (74) sts.]

**Row 30 (dec row):** Work in same way as given for Back to the last 10 sts, inc in each of the next 2 sts, k1, k2tog, k2, sl 1, k1, psso, k1. [51 (65) sts.]

### 2nd size

**Row 16 (dec row):** Work in same way as given for Back to the last 2 sts, k2. [66 sts.]

**Row 30 (dec row):** Work in same way as given for Back to the last 2 sts, k2. [58 sts.]

### All sizes

Cont until all 47 patt rows have been worked.

**Eyelet and dec row:** With A, k1, [(k2tog, yo) twice, k3tog, yo] 7 (8:9) times, k1. [44 (50:56) sts.]

**Next row:** With A, purl. Cont in st st and A beg with a knit row, inc 1 st at side edge on the 7th (7th:9th) and 5 foll 8th (9th:9th) rows [50 (56:62) sts], then work straight until Front measures same as Back to beg of armhole shaping, ending with a WS row.

## Shape armhole and front edge

Cast off 6 (7:9) sts at beg of the next row, knit to the last 2 sts, k2tog. [43 (48:52) sts.] Purl 1 row. (Dec 1 st at each end of the next

row, then 1 st at armhole edge on the next row) 2 (2:3) times. [37 (42:43) sts.] Dec 1 st at each end of the next row. [35 (40:41) sts.]

### 2nd and 3rd sizes

Dec 1 st at each end of the 2 foll alt rows. [36 (37) sts.]

### All sizes

Keeping armhole edge straight, cont to dec 1 st at front edge on the 2 (0:0) foll alt rows, then the 9 (10:10) foll 4th rows [24 (26:27) sts], then work straight until Front measures same as Back to beg of shoulder shaping, ending with a WS row.

### Shape shoulder

Cast off 6 sts at beg of the next row, 6 (6:7) sts
on the foll alt row, 6 (7:7) sts on the foll alt
row. Work 1 row. Cast off rem 6 (7:7) sts.

## RIGHT FRONT

Work as given for Left Front placing patt as
follows:

*1st and 3rd sizes*

**Row 1:** With A, purl.

**Row 2:** With A, k1, k2tog, k6, *inc in each of
the next 2 sts, k6, sl 1, k1, psso, k2tog, k6; rep
from * to last 2 sts, inc in next st, k1.

*2nd size*

Work as given for Back.

*All sizes*

Complete as given for Left Front, reversing
shapings.

## SLEEVES (MAKE 2)

With 4 mm needles and A, cast on 66 sts. Purl
3 rows.

**Row 1:** With A, purl.

**Row 2:** With A, k1, inc in next st, k5, sl 1, k1,
psso, k2tog, k5, *inc in each of next 2 sts, k5,
sl 1, k1, psso, k2tog, k5; rep from * to last
2 sts, inc in next st, k1.

**Row 3:** With A, purl.

Cont in patt as given for Back but in stripe
sequence as follows:

Work 4 more rows in A, 4 rows in B, 2 rows in
C, 2 rows in A.

**Row 16 (dec row):** With A, k1, inc in next st,
k1, k2tog, k2, sl 1, k1, psso, k2tog, k2, k2tog,
k1, *inc in each of next 2 sts, k1, k2tog, k2,
sl 1, k1, psso, k2tog, k2, k2tog, k1; rep from
* to last 2 sts, inc in next st, k1. [58 sts.]

**Row 17:** With A, purl.

**Row 18:** With A, k1, inc in next st, k4, sl 1,
k1, psso, k2tog, k4, *inc in each of next 2 sts,
k4, sl 1, k1, psso, k2tog, k4; rep from * to last
2 sts, inc in next st, k1.

Work 3 more rows in A, 4 rows in B, 2 rows in
C, 3 rows in A.

**Dec row:** With A, p1 (3:3), *p2tog, p4 (5:8);
rep from * 9 (7:5) times, p2tog, p1 (4:3). [48
(50:52) sts.]

**Eyelet row:** K2 (1:2), *k2tog, yon; rep from
* to last 2 (1:2) sts, k2 (1:2).

**Next row:** With A, purl.

Cont in A and st st beg with a knit row, at the
same time inc 1 st at each end of the
16 (17:19) foll 5th rows. [80 (84:90) sts.] Cont
straight until sleeve measures 34 (36:36) cm
(13½ (14:14) in) from top of eyelet row, ending
with a WS row.

### Shape sleeve top

Cast off 6 (7:9) sts at beg of the next 2 rows
[68 (70:72) sts], then dec 1 st at each end of
the next 10 rows [48 (50:52) sts], then on the
3 (4:5) foll 4th rows [42 (42:42) sts], then on
the next 12 rows. [18 sts.] Cast off.

## BUTTON BAND

With 3¼ mm needles and A, cast on 7 sts.
Cont in rib as follows:
**Row 1:** RS. K1, (k1b, p1) twice, k1b, k1.
**Row 2:** K1, (p1, k1b) 3 times.
Cont in rib as set until band (when slightly stretched) fits up left front to beg of front edge shaping, ending with a 2nd rib row.

### Shape collar

Rib 3, k1, p1 into back of loop between st just knitted and next st, rib to end.
Work 3 rows without inc.
Rep the last 4 rows until there are 37 sts ending at straight edge (opposite side to incs). Cast off 10 sts, return st on RH needle to LH needle, recast on 10 sts using cable method (insert RH needle between first two sts on LH needle, yon, place loop onto LH needle). Cont without further shaping until collar fits to centre of back neck. Cast off ribwise. Sl st into place.
Place markers for buttons, the first 2 cm (¾ in) up from cast-on edge the last 2 cm (¾ in) down from beg of front edge shaping and the remainder spaced evenly between.

## BUTTONHOLE BAND

Work as given for Button Band making buttonholes to correspond with markers on Button Band as follows:-
**Row 1:** RS. Rib 3, (yon) twice, k2tog-tbl, rib 2.

**Row 2:** Rib across row dropping one of the (yon) loops.
Complete as given for Button Band.

### Shape collar

Rib to last 3 sts, p1 and k1 into back of loop between st just knitted and next st, p1, k1b, k1. [9 sts.]

## TO MAKE UP

Press as instructions on ball band.
Join shoulders. Join collar seam at centre of back neck then sew to back neck. Sew sleeve tops into armholes then join side and sleeve seams. Thread ribbon through eyelet holes on waist and sleeves.

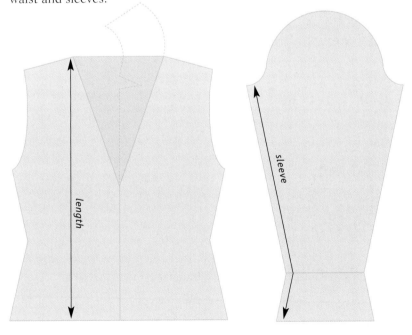

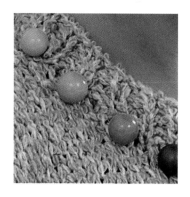

*This cardigan is worked in an unusual ribbon yarn and using a simple stocking stitch, which is very easy to work and creates a fabric in no time. The beads round the neckline make this a really pretty garment.*

# CARDIGAN WITH BEADS

★☆☆ VERY EASY

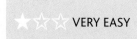 *Stocking stitch is one of the easiest knitted fabrics to create.*

## MEASUREMENTS

### To fit bust

| | | | | | | |
|---|---|---|---|---|---|---|
| 81 | 86 | 91 | 97 | 102 | 107 | cm |
| 32 | 34 | 36 | 38 | 40 | 42 | in |

### Actual width

| | | | | | | |
|---|---|---|---|---|---|---|
| 85 | 91 | 97 | 102 | 108 | 114 | cm |
| 33½ | 36 | 38 | 40 | 42½ | 45 | in |

### Actual length

| | | | | | | |
|---|---|---|---|---|---|---|
| 58 | 60 | 61 | 62 | 64 | 66 | cm |
| 22¼ | 23¾ | 24 | 24½ | 25¼ | 26 | in |

### Actual sleeve seam

| | | | | | | |
|---|---|---|---|---|---|---|
| 43 | 46 | 46 | 46 | 46 | 47 | cm |
| 17 | 18 | 18 | 18 | 18 | 18½ | in |

*In the instructions figures are given for the smallest size first; larger sizes follow in brackets. Where only one set of figures is given this applies to all sizes.*

## MATERIALS

- 11 (12:13:14:15:16) × 50 g balls of Rowan Cotton Braid in 352
- Pair each of 7 mm and 8 mm needles
- Stitch holders
- Large beads for decoration round neck
- 7 buttons for fastening

## TENSION

10½ sts and 17 rows to 10 cm (4 in) measured over stocking stitch using 8 mm needles.

## ABBREVIATIONS

*See page 10.*

# CARDIGAN

## BACK

With 7 mm needles cast on 45 (47:51:54:57:59) sts.
**Row 1:** RS. *K1, p1; rep from * to last st, k1.
**Row 2:** *P1, k1; rep from * to last st, p1.
Rep these 2 rows 2 times more inc 0 (1:0:0:0:1) sts in centre on last row. [45 (48:51:54:57:60) sts.]
Change to 8 mm needles. Cont in st st beg with a knit row shaping sides by dec 1 st at each end of the 5th and 3 foll 6th rows, then inc 1 st at each end of the foll 8th and 3 foll 6th rows. [45 (48:51:54:57:60) sts.] Cont straight until work measures 39 (41:41:41:42:43) cm (15½ (16:16:16:16½:17) in) from beg, ending with a WS row.

### Shape armholes

Cast off 3 (3:4:4:5:5) sts at beg of the next 2 rows [39 (42:43:46:47:50) sts], then dec 1 st at each end of the 2 (2:2:3:3:3) foll alt rows. [35 (38:39:40:41:44) sts.] Cont straight until armhole measures 19 (19:20:21:22:23) cm [7½ (7½:8:8¼:8¾:9) in) from beg of shaping, ending with a WS row.

*Plain knitted sweaters and cardigans look wonderful when embellished wtih interesting buttons, beads, ribbons, sequins or embroidery.*

### Shape shoulders and back neck

Cast off 3 (4:4:4:4:4) sts at beg of the next row, knit until there are 11 (11:11:11:12:13) sts on right hand needle after cast off, turn and work on these sts for first side. Leave rem sts on a st holder.

Work 3 rows dec 1 st at neck edge on each row and casting off 4 (4:4:4:4:5) sts for shoulder on the 2nd row. Cast off rem 4 (4:4:4:5:5) sts.

With RS facing, leave the centre 7 (8:9:10:9:10) sts on a st holder, rejoin yarn and knit rem 14 (15:15:15:16:17) sts. Complete this side to match first side, reversing shapings.

### LEFT FRONT

With 7 mm needles cast on 21 (23:25:27:27:29) sts and work 6 rows in rib as given for Back welt inc 1 (1:0:0:1:1) sts in centre on last row. [22 (24:25:27:28:30) sts.]

Change to 8 mm needles. Cont in st st beg with a knit row shaping side by dec 1 st at RH edge on the 5th and 3 foll 6th rows [18 (20:21:23:24:26) sts], then inc 1 st at same edge on the foll 8th and 3 foll 6th rows. [22 (24:25:27:28:30) sts.]

Cont straight until Front measures same as Back to beg of armhole shaping, ending with a WS row.

### Shape armhole

Cast off 3 (3:4:4:5:5) sts at beg of the next row [19 (21:21:23:23:25) sts], then dec 1 st at same edge on the 2 (2:2:3:3:3) foll alt rows. [17 (19:19:20:20:22) sts.] Cont straight until work measures 13 rows shorter than Back to beg of shoulder shaping, ending with a RS row.

### Shape neck

Cast off 3 (4:4:5:4:5) sts at beg of the next row [14 (15:15:15:16:17) sts], then dec 1 st at neck edge on the 3 foll alt rows. Work 6 rows straight ending at armhole edge. [11 (12:12:12:13:14) sts.]

### Shape shoulder

Cast off 3 (4:4:4:4:4) sts at beg of the next row, 4 (4:4:4:4:5) sts on the foll alt row. Work 1 row. Cast off rem 4 (4:4:4:5:5) sts.

### RIGHT FRONT

Work as given for Left Front, reversing shapings.

### SLEEVES (MAKE 2)

With 7 mm needles cast on 21 (21:23:23:25:25) sts and work 6 rows in rib as given for Back welt.

Change to 8 mm needles. Cont in st st beg with a knit row, at the same time inc 1 st at each end of the 7th (5th:5th:5th:5th:5th) row and 6 (1:1:1:5:7) foll 8th (6th:6th:6th:6th:6th) rows [35 (25:27:27:37:41) sts], then on the

0 (6:6:6:3:2) foll 0th (8th:8th:8th:8th:8th)
rows. [35 (37:39:39:43:45) sts.] Cont straight
until Sleeve measures 43 (46:46:46:46:47) cm
(17 (18:18:18:18:18½) in) from beg, ending
with a WS row.

### Shape sleeve top
Cast off 3 (3:4:4:5:5) sts at beg of the next 2
rows [29 (31:31:31:33:35) sts], then dec 1 st
at each end of the next and 7 (7:8:8:9:9) foll
alt rows [13 (15:13:13:13:15) sts], then on the
next 3 rows. [7 (9:7:7:7:9) sts.] Cast off.

### NECKBAND
Join shoulders.
With RS facing and 7 mm needles, knit up
17 (18:18:19:19:20) sts from right front neck
edge, 3 sts from right back neck, working
across st holder for back neck, k7 (8:9:10:9:
10) sts from back neck dec 0 (1:0:1:0:1) sts in
centre of these sts, knit up 3 sts from left back
neck and 17 (18:18:19:19:20) sts down left
front neck. [47 (49:51:53:53:55) sts.]
Work 5 rows in rib as given for back welt. Cast
off in rib.

### BUTTON BAND
With 7 mm needles cast on 6 sts and cont in
rib as follows:
**Row 1:** RS. Sl 1, (k1, p1) twice, k1b.
Rep this row until band fits up left front to top
of neckband. Cast off in rib. Sew in place.

Mark the position of 7 buttons, the first
1.5 cm (¾ in) up from cast-on edge, the last
1.5cm (¾ in) down from top of neckband and
the remainder spaced evenly between.

### BUTTONHOLE BAND
With 7 mm needles cast on
6 sts and cont in rib as button band making
buttonholes to correspond with markers as
follows:
**Buttonhole row 1:** RS. Sl 1, k1, cast off next
st, rib to end.
**Buttonhole row 2:** In rib casting on over cast
of st on previous row.

### TO MAKE UP
Sew sleeve heads into armholes then join
side and sleeve seams. Sew on buttons.
Sew on beads.

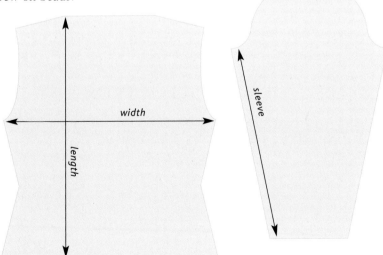

*This lovely sweater is knitted using a textured yarn and has a panel of knit/purl diagonal stitches on the front and back. The bell edging detail on the cuffs and lower hem make this a pretty, feminine sweater.*

# SWEATER WITH FRILLED HEM AND CUFFS

★★☆ EASY

*Creating the frilled edges requires some skill.*

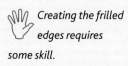
*The diagonal stitch pattern requires concentration.*

## MEASUREMENTS
### To fit bust

| | | | | | |
|---|---|---|---|---|---|
| 81 | 86 | 91 | 97 | 102 | cm |
| 32 | 34 | 36 | 38 | 40 | in |

### Actual width

| | | | | | |
|---|---|---|---|---|---|
| 88 | 93 | 98 | 103 | 108 | cm |
| 34¾ | 36¾ | 38½ | 40½ | 42½ | in |

### Actual length

| | | | | | |
|---|---|---|---|---|---|
| 53 | 53 | 54 | 55 | 56 | cm |
| 21 | 21 | 21¼ | 21¾ | 22 | in |

### Actual sleeve seam

| | | | | | |
|---|---|---|---|---|---|
| 44 | 47 | 47 | 47 | 47 | cm |
| 17½ | 18½ | 18½ | 18½ | 18½ | in |

*In the instructions figures are given for the smallest size first; larger sizes follow in brackets. Where only one set of figures is given this applies to all sizes.*

## MATERIALS
- 9 (9:10:10:11) × 50 g hanks of Rowan Summer Tweed in 508
- Pair of 5 mm needles
- Stitch holders

## TENSION
16 sts and 23 rows to 10 cm (4 in) measured over stocking stitch using 5 mm needles.

## ABBREVIATIONS
*See page 10.*

# SWEATER

## BACK AND FRONT (ALIKE)
With 5 mm needles cast on 207 (219:231:243:255) sts and work bell edge patt as follows:

**Rows 1 and 3:** RS. P3, *k9, p3; rep from * to end.

**Rows 2 and 4:** K3, *p9, k3; rep from * to end.

**Row 5:** P3, *yb, sl 1, k1, psso, k5, k2tog, p3; rep from * to end.

**Rows 6 and 8:** K3, *p7, k3; rep from * to end.

**Row 7:** P3, *k7, p3; rep from * to end.

**Row 9:** P3, *yb, sl 1, k1, psso, k3, k2tog, p3; rep from * to end.

**Rows 10 and 12:** K3, *p5, k3; rep from * to end.

**Row 11:** P3, *k5, p3; rep from * to end.

**Row 13:** P3, *yb, sl 1, k1, psso, k1, k2tog, p3; rep from * to end.

**Rows 14 and 16:** K3, *p3, k3; rep from * to end.

**Row 15:** P3, *k3, p3; rep from * to end.

**Row 17:** P3, *yb, sl 1, k2tog, psso, p3; rep from * to end.

**Row 18:** K3, *p1, k3; rep from * to end.

These 18 rows form the bell edge.
[71 (75:79:83:87) sts.]

Cont as follows:

**Row 1:** K19 (21:23:25:27), p1, k1b, (p2, k2) 7 times, p1, k1b, p1, k19 (21:23:25:27).

**Row 2:** P19 (21:23:25:27), k1, p1, k2, (p2, k2) 6 times, p2, k1, p1, k1, p19 (21:23:25:27).

**Row 3:** K19 (21:23:25:27), p1, k1b, (k2, p2) 7 times, k1, k1b, p1, k19 (21:23:25:27).

**Row 4:** P19 (21:23:25:27), k1, p3, (k2, p2) 7 times, k1, p19 (21:23:25:27).

These 4 rows form the patt. Cont in patt until work measures 34 cm (13½ in) from beg, ending with a WS row.

**Shape armholes**

Cast off 3 (3:4:4:5) sts at beg of the next 2 rows [65 (69:71:75:77) sts], then dec 1 st at each end of the 5 (5:6:6:7) foll alt rows. [55 (59:59:63:63) sts.]

Cont straight in patt until armhole measures 15 (15:16:17:18) cm (6 (6:6¼:6½:7) in) from beg of shaping, ending with a WS row.

**Shape neck**

K18 (19:19:20:20), turn and leave rem sts on a st holder, work on these sts for first side. Work 10 rows, dec 1 st at neck edge on every row. Work 1 row. Cast off rem 8 (9:9:10:10) sts.

With RS facing, slip the centre 19 (21:21:23:23) sts on a st holder, rejoin yarn and patt to end. Complete this side to match first side, reversing shapings.

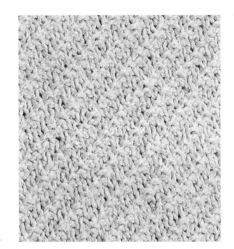

## SLEEVES (MAKE 2)

With 5 mm needles cast on 87 (87:99:99:111) sts and work the 18 rows of bell edge as given for Back. [31 (31:35:35:39) sts.]

Cont in st st beg with a knit row, at the same time inc 1 st at each end of the 3rd and 3 foll 4th rows [39 (39:43:43:47) sts], then on the 8 (9:9:9:9) foll 8th rows. [55 (57:61:61:65) sts.] Cont straight until sleeve measures 44 (47:47:47:47) cm (17½ (18½:18½:18½:18½) in) from beg, ending with a WS row.

### Shape sleeve top

Cast off 3 (3:4:4:5) sts at beg of the next 2 rows [49 (51:53:53:55) sts], then dec 1 st at each end of the next and 8 (7:8:8:11) foll alt rows [31 (35:35:35:31) sts], then on the next 9 (11:11:11:9) rows. Cast off rem 13 sts.

## NECKBAND

Join left shoulder.

With 5 mm needles, knit up 9 sts down right back neck, knit across 19 (21:21:23:23) sts from st holder, knit up 9 sts up left back neck, 9 sts down left front neck, knit across 19 (21:21:23:23) sts from st holder, knit up 9 sts up right front neck.

[74 (78:78:82:82) sts.] Knit 1 row. Cast off.

## TO MAKE UP

Join right shoulder.

Sew sleeve tops into armholes then join side and sleeve seams.

## HELPFUL HINT

*When measuring your work, lay the pieces out on a flat surface and smooth out, without stretching. This will guarantee accurate measurements.*

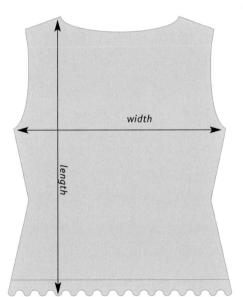

*Knitted in a chunky yarn this three-quarter-sleeved top is knitted in stocking stitch with a pretty leaf and bobble border. The lace-effect detail round the neck and the ribbon tie is a delightful added touch.*

# SCOOP-NECKED TOP WITH LACY EDGING

★ ★ ☆ EASY

 *The basic stitch and pattern is easy but the leaf and bobble pattern around the edges requires some skill and concentration.*

## MEASUREMENTS

**To fit bust**

| 81 | 86 | 91 | 97 | 102 | 107 | cm |
|----|----|----|----|-----|-----|-----|
| 32 | 34 | 36 | 38 | 40 | 42 | in |

**Actual width**

| 82 | 85 | 92 | 98 | 105 | 111 | cm |
|----|----|----|----|-----|-----|-----|
| 32¼ | 33½ | 36¼ | 38½ | 41½ | 43¾ | in |

**Actual length**

| 56 | 57 | 58 | 59 | 59 | 61 | cm |
|----|----|----|----|----|----|-----|
| 22 | 22½ | 22¾ | 23¼ | 23¼ | 24 | in |

**Actual sleeve seam**

| 25 | 27 | 27 | 27 | 28 | 28 | cm |
|----|----|----|----|----|----|-----|
| 9¾ | 10¾ | 10¾ | 10¾ | 11 | 11 | in |

*In the instructions figures are given for the smallest size first; larger sizes follow in brackets. Where only one set of figures is given this applies to all sizes.*

## MATERIALS

- 4 (4:5:5:6:6) × 100 g balls of Sirdar Denim Chunky in Lilac Frost 564
- Pair each of 5½ mm and 6½ mm needles
- 5½ mm circular needle
- Stitch holder
- Ribbon

## TENSION

14 sts and 19 rows to 10 cm (4 in) measured over stocking stitch using 6½ needles.

## ABBREVIATIONS

**MB** – Make bobble: (k1,yo,k1,yo,k1) into one st, turn, p5, turn, k5, turn, p1, p3tog, p1, turn, sl 1, k2tog, psso, completing bobble.
*See also page 10.*

# SWEATER

## BACK

Using 6½ mm needles cast on 58 (60:65:69:74:78) sts.

Work 4 rows in st st beg with a knit row.

*Leaf patterned border*

**Row 1:** RS. K3 (4:3:5:4:6), p1; *MB, p1, k4, p1, rep from * to last 5 (6:5:7:6:8) sts, MB, p1, k3 (4:3:5:4:6).

**Row 2:** Purl, working p1b in top of MB.

**Row 3:** K3 (4:3:5:4:6), p1; *(k1, yo, k1) in next st, p1, k4, p1, rep from * to last 5 (6:5:7:6:8) sts, (k1, yo, k1) in next st, p1, k3 (4:3:5:4:6).

**Row 4 and all other WS rows:** Work sts as they appear on needle.

**Row 5:** K3 (4:3:5:4:6), p1, *k1, (k1, yo, k1) in next st, k1, p1, k4, p1; rep from * to last 7 (8:7:9:8:10) sts, k1, (k1, yo, k1) in next st, k1, p1, k3 (4:3:5:4:6).

**Row 7:** K3 (4:3:5:4:6), p1, *k2, (k1, yo, k1) in next st, k2, p1, k4, p1; rep from * to last 9 (10:9:11:10:12) sts, k2, (k1, yo, k1) in next st, k2, p1, k3 (4:3:5:4:6).

**Row 9:** K3 (4:3:5:4:6), p1, *k7, p1, k4, p1; rep from * to last 11 (12:11:13:12:14) sts, k7, p1, k3 (4:3:5:4:6).

**Row 11:** K3 (4:3:5:4:6), p1, *sl 1, k1, psso, k3, k2tog, p1, k4, p1; rep from * to last 11 (12:11:13:12:14) sts, sl 1, k1, psso, k3, k2tog, p1, k3 (4:3:5:4:6).

**Row 13:** K3 (4:3:5:4:6), p1, *sl 1, k1, psso, k1, k2tog, p1, k4, p1; rep from * to last 9 (10:9:11:10:12) sts, sl 1, k1, psso, k1, k2tog, p1, k3 (4:3:5:4:6).

**Row 15:** K3 (4:3:5:4:6), p1, *sl 1, k2tog, psso, p1, k4, p1; rep from * to last 7 (8:7:9:8:10) sts, sl 1, k2tog, psso, p1, k3 (4:3:5:4:6).

**Row 16:** As Row 4.

Cont in st st beg with a knit row until work measures 30 (30:30:31:31:31) cm (12 (12:12:12¼:12¼:12¼) in) from beg, ending with a WS row. **

### Shape raglan

Cast off 3 (3:3:3:4:4) sts at beg of the next 2 rows. [52 (54:59:63:66:70) sts.]

*1st, 2nd, 3rd and 4th sizes only*

Work 12 (12:8:4) rows dec 1 st at both ends of the next and every foll 4th (4th:4th:0th) row. [46 (48:55:61) sts.]

*All sizes*

Work 12 (14:20:24:28:32) rows dec 1 st at both ends of the next and every foll alt row, 34 (34:35:37:38:38) sts. Cast off rem sts.

### FRONT

Work as given for Back to **.

### Shape raglan

Cast off 3 (3:3:3:4:4) sts at beg of the next 2 rows. [52 (54:59:63:66:70) sts.]

*1st, 2nd, 3rd and 4th sizes only*

Work 12 (12:8:4) rows dec 1 st at both ends of the next and every foll 4th (4th:4th:0th) row. [46 (48:55:61) sts.]

*All sizes*

Work 4 (6:12:16:20:24) rows dec 1 st at both ends of the next and every foll alt row. [42 (42:43:45:46:46) sts.]

### Shape neck

**Next row:** K2tog, k7, turn and leave rem 33 (33:34:36:37:37) sts on a st holder. Working on these 8 sts only proceed as follows:

**Next row:** Purl.

Work 5 rows dec 1 st at both ends of the next and every foll alt row. [2 sts.]

**Next row:** P2tog.

Fasten off.

With RS facing, rejoin yarn to rem 33 (33:34:36:37:37) sts, cast off 24 (24:25:27:28:28) sts, knit to last 2 sts, k2tog. [8 sts.] Complete to match first side of neck.

### SLEEVES (MAKE 2)

Using 5½ mm needles cast on 38 (38:42:42:46:46) sts, work 5 cm (2 in) in

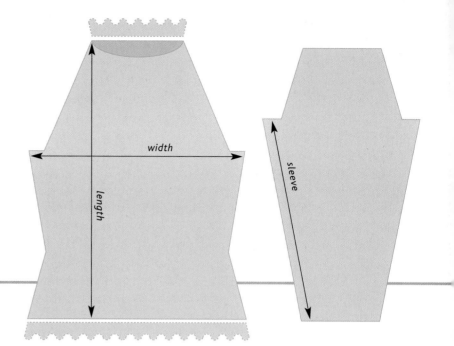

*width*

*length*

*sleeve*

rib as follows, ending with a WS row:

**Row 1:** RS. *K2, p2; rep from * to last
2 sts, k2.

**Row 2:** *P2, k2; rep from * to last 2 sts, p2.
Change to 6½ mm needles. Cont in st st beg
with a knit row, inc 1 st at both ends of the 5th
and every foll 6th (6th:6th:6th:7th:7th) row to
50 (50:54:54:58:58) sts.

Cont without shaping until sleeve measures
25 (27:27:27:28:28) cm
(9¾ (10¾:10¾:10¾:11:11) in) or length
required, ending with a WS row.

### Shape raglan

Cast off 3 (3:3:3:4:4) sts at beg of the next
2 rows. [44 (44:48:48:50:50) sts.]
Work 8 (12:8:8:4:12) rows dec 1 st at both
ends of the next and every foll 4th (4th:4th:
4th:0th:4th) row. [40 (38:44:44:48:44) sts.]
Work 16 (14:20:20:24:20) rows dec 1 st at
both ends of the next and every foll alt row.
Cast off rem 24 sts.

### NECKBAND

With 5½ mm needles and using the thumb
method, cast on 211
(211:211:222:222:222) sts.

**Row 1:** RS. Purl.

**Row 2:** K2, *k1, slip this st back onto LH
needle, lift the next 8 sts on LH needle over
this st and off needle, (yf) twice, knit the first
st again, k2; rep from * to end.

**Row 3:** K1, *p2tog, drop loop of 2 sts made in
previous row and (k1, k1b) twice, into it, p1;
rep from * to last st, k1. ***
[116 (116:116:122:122:122) sts.]
Knit 2 rows.

**Eyelet row:** K4 (4:4:2:2:2), * yf, k2tog, k2; rep
from * to end.
Purl 3 rows. Cast off knitwise.

### LOWER BORDER

With 5½ mm circular needle and using the
thumb method, cast on 211
(222:233:244:255:266) sts and work as given
for Neckband to ***.
[116 (122:128:134:140:146) sts.]
Knit 4 rows. Cast off knitwise.

### TO MAKE UP

Join raglans then side and sleeve seams.
Beginning at centre back, sew Neckband to
neck edge and Lower Border to lower edge
beginning at side seam. Join short ends.
Thread ribbon in and out of eyelets on
neckband and tie in a bow at centre of front
neck. Pin out garment to the measurement
given on page 96. Cover with damp cloths and
leave until dry.

*Keep the chill off with this simple V-necked slipover. It is made using a chenille yarn to give a luxurious look and is worked in stocking stitch with subtle striped colour changes.*

# STRIPED SLEEVELESS TOP

★★☆ EASY

 *This simple garment requires some skill when it comes to picking up stitches for the armholes.*

## MEASUREMENTS

**To fit bust**

| 81 | 86 | 91 | 97 | 102 | cm |
| 32 | 34 | 36 | 38 | 40 | in |

**Actual width**

| 81 | 86 | 91 | 97 | 102 | cm |
| 32 | 34 | 36 | 38 | 40 | in |

**Actual length**

| 55 | 56 | 57 | 58 | 59 | cm |
| 21½ | 22 | 22½ | 23 | 23¼ | in |

*In the instructions figures are given for the smallest size first; larger sizes follow in brackets. Where only one set of figures is given this applies to all sizes.*

## MATERIALS

- 2 (2:2:3:3) × 100 g balls of Rowan Chunky Cotton Chenille in Angel Tears 391 (A)
- 1 (1:1:2:2) × 100 g balls of Rowan Chunky Cotton Chenille in Flutter 389 (B)
- 1 (1:1:2:2) × 100 g balls of Rowan Chunky Cotton Chenille in Wraith 394 (C)
- Pair each of 4 mm and 5 mm needles
- Stitch holder
- Safety pin

## TENSION

15 sts and 26 rows to 10 cm (4 in) measured over stocking stitch using 5 mm needles.

## ABBREVIATIONS

**2tog-tbl** – work 2 stitches together through back of loops
*See also page 10.*

## SLEEVELESS TOP

### BACK

With 4 mm needles and A, cast on 61 (65:69:73:77) sts.
**Row 1:** RS *k1, p1; rep from * to last st, k1.
**Row 2:** *P1, k1; rep from * to last st, p1.
These 2 rows form the rib; work 4 more rows in rib.
Change to 5 mm needles. Cont in st st beg with a knit row and stripe patt, at the same time, shaping for sides as given below:
**Stripe sequence:** Work 6 rows in A, 4 rows in B, (2 rows in A, 2 rows in C), twice, 2 rows in A, 4 rows in B. These 24 rows form the patt and are repeated throughout. Cont in patt dec 1 st at both ends of the 5th and 4 foll 4th rows [51 (55:59:63:67) sts], then inc 1 st at both ends of the foll 12th and 4 foll 8th rows. [61 (65:69:73:77) sts.]
Cont straight in patt until work measures 35 cm (13¾ in) from beg, ending with a WS row. **

## Shape armholes

Cast off 4 (4:5:5:6) sts at beg of the next
2 rows [53 (57:59:63:65) sts], then dec
1 st at both ends of the next 4 rows
[45 (49:51:55:57) sts], then on the 3 foll alt
rows. [39 (43:45:49:51) sts.]
Cont straight in patt until armhole measures
20 (21:22:23:24) cm (8 (8¼:8½:9:9½) in) from
beg, ending with a WS row.

## Shape shoulders and back of neck

Cast off 3 (4:4:5:5) sts at beg of the next row,
knit until there are 8 (9:9:10:10) sts on RH
needle after cast-off. Work on these sts for
first side. Cast off 4 sts at neck edge on next
row. Cast off rem 4 (5:5:6:6) sts.
With RS facing, slip the centre
17 (17:19:19:21) sts on a st holder, rejoin yarn
and knit to end. Complete as given for first
side, reversing shapings.

## FRONT

Work as given for Back to **.

## Shape armholes and divide for V-neck

Cast off 4 (4:5:5:6) sts at beg of the next row,
knit until there are 26 (28:29:31:32) sts on
RH needle after cast-off. Turn and work on
these sts for first side.

Dec 1 st at beg of the next row. Work 10 rows dec 1 st at neck edge on the 2 foll 4th rows, at the same time, dec 1 st at armhole edge on the next 4 rows and 3 foll alt rows. [16 (18:19:21:22) sts.]
Keeping armhole edge straight, cont to dec 1 st at neck edge on every 4th row to 7 (9:9:11:11) sts, then work straight until Front matches Back to beg of shoulder shaping, ending with a WS row.

### Shape shoulder
Cast off 3 (4:4:5:5) sts at beg of the next row. Work 1 row. Cast off rem 4 (5:5:6:6) sts. With RS facing, slip the centre st onto a safety pin (this marks the st), rejoin yarn and knit to end. Complete this side to match first side, reversing shapings.

### NECKBAND
Join left shoulder. With RS facing, 4 mm needles and A, knit up 3 sts from right back neck, knit across 17 (17:19:19:21) sts from back neck st holder, dec 1 st in centre of these sts, knit up 3 sts from left back neck, 35 (37:39:41:43) sts down left front neck, knit marked st, knit up 35 (37:39:41:43) sts up right front neck. [93 (97:103:107:113) sts.]
**Next row:** Beg with a 2nd rib row, rib to within 2 sts of marked st, p2tog, p1, p2tog-tbl, rib rem 55 (57:61:63:67) sts.

**Next row:** Rib to within 2 sts of marked st, k2tog-tbl, k1b, k2tog, rib to end.
Rib 3 more rows, dec either side of marked st as set. [83 (87:93:97:103) sts.] Cast off ribwise, dec as before.

### ARMBANDS (MAKE 2)
Join right shoulder and neckband.
With RS facing, 4 mm needles and A, knit up 81 (85:89:93:97) sts evenly along one armhole edge. Beg with a 2nd rib row, rib 5 rows. Cast off ribwise.

### TO MAKE UP
Join side seams.

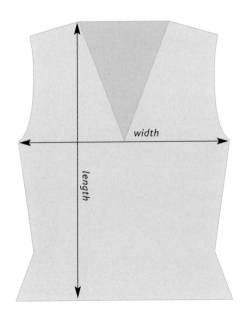

*This luxurious kid mohair cardigan is gorgeously cosy and can be teamed with anything. It is worked in simple stocking stitch and has pretty heart-shaped buttons.*

# SILKY MOHAIR CARDIGAN

★☆☆ VERY EASY

*Another easy-to-knit garment created in stocking stitch and with very simple shaping.*

*ake care when working with mohair as the yarn tends to shed.*

## MEASUREMENTS

| | | | | | |
|---|---|---|---|---|---|
| **To fit bust** | | | | | |
| 81 | 86 | 91 | 97 | 102 | cm |
| 32 | 34 | 36 | 38 | 40 | in |
| **Actual width** | | | | | |
| 86 | 91 | 96 | 101 | 106 | cm |
| 34 | 36 | 37¾ | 39¾ | 41¾ | in |
| **Actual length** | | | | | |
| 45 | 46 | 47 | 48 | 49 | cm |
| 17¾ | 18 | 18½ | 19 | 19¼ | in |
| **Actual sleeve seam** | | | | | |
| 43 | 43 | 46 | 46 | 46 | cm |
| 17 | 17 | 18 | 18 | 18 | in |

*In the instructions figures are given for the smallest size first; larger sizes follow in brackets. Where only one set of figures is given this applies to all sizes.*

## MATERIALS

- 8 (9:10:11:12) × 25 g balls of Rowan Kidsilk Haze in 581
- Pair each of 3 mm and 3¾ mm needles
- Stitch holder
- 7 small buttons

## TENSION

23 sts and 32 rows to 10 cm (4 in) measured over stocking stitch using 3¾ mm needles and yarn used double.

## ABBREVIATIONS

*See page 10.*

# CARDIGAN

## BACK

With 3 mm needles and yarn used double throughout, cast on 99 (105:111:117:123) sts.

**Row 1:** RS. *K1, p1; rep from * to last st, k1.

**Row 2:** *P1, k1; rep from * to last st, p1.

Rep these 2 rows 3 times more.

Change to 3¾ mm needles. Cont in st st beg with a knit row until work measures 26 (27:27:27:27) cm (10¼ (10¾:10¾:10¾:10¾) in) from beg, ending with a WS row.

### Shape armholes

Cast off 6 (6:7:7:9) sts at beg of the next 2 rows [87 (93:97:103:105) sts], then dec 1 st at each end of the next 4 rows [79 (85:89:95:97) sts], then on the 2 (2:2:4:4) foll alt rows. [75 (81:85:87:89) sts.]

Cont straight until armhole measures 19 (19:20:21:22) cm (7½ (7½:8:8¼:8¾) in) from beg of shaping, ending with a WS row.

### Shape shoulders and back neck

Cast off 7 (8:8:8:9) sts at beg of the next 2 rows. [61 (65:69:71:71) sts.] Cast off 7 (8:9:9:9) sts at beg of the next row, knit until there are 11 (12:13:13:13) sts on RH needle, turn and leave rem sts on a st holder. Work on

these sts for first side. Cast off 4 sts at beg of
the next row. Cast off rem 7 (8:9:9:9) sts.
With RS facing, rejoin yarn and leave centre
25 (25:25:27:27) sts on a st holder. Complete
this side to match first side, reversing
shapings.

### LEFT FRONT

With 3 mm needles and yarn used double
throughout, cast on 49 (51:55:57:61) sts and
work 8 rows in rib as given for Back welt, inc
0 (1:0:1:0) st in centre of last row.
[49 (52:55:58:61) sts.]
Change to 3¾ mm needles. Cont in st st beg
with a knit row, until work measures same as
Back to beg of armhole shaping, ending with a
WS row.

#### Shape armhole

Cast off 6 (6:7:7:9) sts at beg of the next row.
[43 (46:48:51:52) sts.] Work 1 row then dec
1 st at armhole edge on the next 4 rows
[39 (42:44:47:48) sts], then on the 2 (2:2:4:4)
foll alt rows. [37 (40:42:43:44) sts.]
Cont straight until Front measures
23 (23:23:23:25) rows shorter than Back
to beg of shoulder shaping, ending with a
RS row.

#### Shape front neck

Cast off 6 (6:6:7:7) sts at beg of the next row,
then dec 1 st at same edge on the next 3 rows

[28 (31:33:33:34) sts], then on the 7 foll alt
rows. [21 (24:26:26:27) sts.]
Work 5 (5:5:5:7) rows, ending at side edge.

#### Shape shoulder

Cast off 7 (8:8:8:9) sts at beg of the next row,
7 (8:9:9:9) sts on the foll alt row. Work 1 row.
Cast off rem 7 (8:9:9:9) sts.

### RIGHT FRONT

Work as given for Left Front, reversing
shapings.

### SLEEVES (MAKE 2)

With 3 mm needles and yarn used double
throughout, cast on 47 (47:51:51:53) sts and
work 8 rows in rib as given for Back welt.
Change to 3¾ mm needles. Cont in st st beg
with a knit row, at the same time inc 1 st at
each end of the 5th and 2 (7:7:7:15) foll 6th
rows [53 (63:67:67:85) sts], then on the
13 (10:10:10:4) foll 8th rows.
[79 (83:87:87:93) sts.]
Cont straight until sleeve measures
43 (43:46:46:46) cm (17 (17:18:18:18) in)
from beg, ending with a WS row.

#### Shape sleeve top

Cast off 6 (6:7:7:8) sts at beg of the next
2 rows [67 (71:73:73:77) sts], then dec 1 st at
each end of the next 12 rows
[43 (47:49:49:53) sts], then on the 3 (3:4:4:4)

foll 4th rows [37 (41:41:41:45) sts], then on the 3 (3:3:3:4) foll alt rows [31 (35:35:35:37) sts], then on the next 6 rows. [19 (23:23:23:25) sts.]
Cast off.

## NECKBAND

Join shoulders.
With RS facing and 3 mm needles and yarn used double, knit up 30 (30:31:33:34) sts along right front neck, 3 sts from right back neck, knit across 25 (25:25:27:27) sts from back neck st holder, knit up 3 sts from left back neck, and 30 (30:31:33:34) sts along left front neck.
[91 (91:93:99:101) sts.]
Beg with a 2nd rib row and work 7 rows in rib. Cast off ribwise.

## BUTTON BAND

With 3 mm needles and yarn used double, cast on 7 sts. Cont in rib as given for Back welt until band fits up left front to top of neckband. Cast off ribwise.
Sew in place then mark the positions of 7 buttons, the first to come 1 cm (½ in) up from cast-on edge the last 1 cm (½ in) down from cast-off edge and the remainder spaced evenly between.

## BUTTONHOLE BAND

Work as given for Button Band making buttonholes to correspond with markers on left front as follows:
**Buttonhole row 1:** RS. Rib 3, (yo) twice, k2tog, rib 2.
**Buttonhole row 2:** Rib, dropping one yo from previous row.

## TO MAKE UP

Sew sleeve tops into armholes then join side and sleeve seams. Sew on buttons.

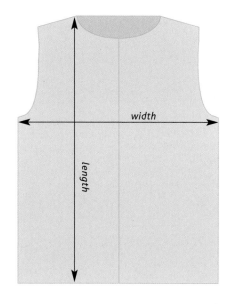

# GLAMOROUS

This chapter is full of lovely items for evenings out, and you don't have to be an expert to create them. They're really versatile to wear – you can relax in style or dress up for an evening out. Sling on the cape teamed with the headband, or the bolero for added warmth, to keep the night time chill at bay, both worked in a luxurious chenille yarn. Or try the textured wrapover cardigan with frilled cuffs. Shimmer and look extra special in the fitted sweater with lace collar and cuffs, worked in a lurex yarn.

*Feel special wearing this simple stocking stitch cape which ties at the front.*

# CAPE AND HEADBAND

★ ☆ ☆ VERY EASY

 *Using large size needles and a thicker yarn means that this garment is really quick and easy to knit up.*

## HELPFUL HINTS

- Always knit chenille yarns by taking the yarn from the 'outside' of the ball.
- To join in a new ball of chenille yarn remove approximately 5 cm (2 in) of chenille from the end of the old and beginning of the new balls by drawing fibres between your thumb-nail and index finger, leaving 5 cm (2 in) of core yarn exposed. Knot these core ends firmly together as close to the remaining chenille as possible and trim the ends.
- When sewing up garments knitted in chenille, use a plain yarn in a matching colour.

## MEASUREMENTS

**To fit bust**

| | | | | | | |
|---|---|---|---|---|---|---|
| 81 | 86 | 91 | 97 | 102 | 107 | cm |
| 32 | 34 | 36 | 38 | 40 | 42 | in |

**Actual width**

| | | | | | | |
|---|---|---|---|---|---|---|
| 130 | 137 | 142 | 150 | 155 | 162 | cm |
| 51¼ | 54 | 56 | 59 | 61 | 63¾ | in |

**Actual length**

| | | | | | | |
|---|---|---|---|---|---|---|
| 35.5 | 35.5 | 35.5 | 38 | 38 | 38 | cm |
| 14 | 14 | 14 | 15 | 15 | 15 | in |

*In the instructions figures are given for the smallest size first; larger sizes follow in brackets. Where only one set of figures is given this applies to all sizes.*

## MATERIALS

- 5 (5:6:6:7:7) × 100 g balls of Sirdar Wow! in Imperial Purple 760
- Pair each of 8 mm and 7 mm needles

## TENSION

8 sts and 15 rows to 10 cm (4 in) measured over stocking stitch using 7 mm needles.

## ABBREVIATIONS

*See page 10.*

# CAPE

### BACK

With 8 mm needles cast on 52 (55:57:60:62:65) sts.
Change to 7 mm needles. Cont in st st beg with a knit row.
Work 6 rows, then dec 1 st at each end of the next and 2 foll 10th rows.
[46 (49:51:54:56:59) sts.]
Dec 1 st on the 1 (1:1:2:2:2) foll 4th rows [44 (47:49:50:52:55) sts], then on the 8 foll alt rows [28 (31:33:34:36:39) sts], then on the next row.
[26 (29:31:32:34:37) sts.]

## Shape shoulders and back neck

**Next row:** K2tog, knit until there are 8 (9:10:10:11:12) sts on RH needle, turn and leave rem sts on a st holder. Dec 1 st at each end of the next 2 rows. [4 (5:6:6:7:8) sts.] Cast off.

With RS facing, rejoin yarn to rem sts, cast off 8 (9:9:10:10:11) sts and knit to last 2 sts, k2tog. Complete this side to match first side, reversing shapings.

## LEFT FRONT

With 8 mm needles cast on 14 (15:16:17:18:19) sts.

Change to 7 mm needles. Cont in st st beg with a knit row.

**Row 1:** Knit.

**Row 2:** Cast on 2 sts, purl these 2 sts then purl to end.

Work 4 rows inc 1 st at front edge on every row. [20 (21:22:23:24:25) sts.]

**Row 7:** Dec 1 st at side edge, inc 1 st at front edge.

Work 2 rows inc 1 st at front edge on every row. [22 (23:24:25:26:27) sts.]

Work 1 row.

Inc 1 st at front edge on the next row. [23 (24:25:26:27:28) sts.]

Work 5 rows straight, place a marker at front edge on last row.

Dec 1 st at side edge on next row.

Work 1 row.

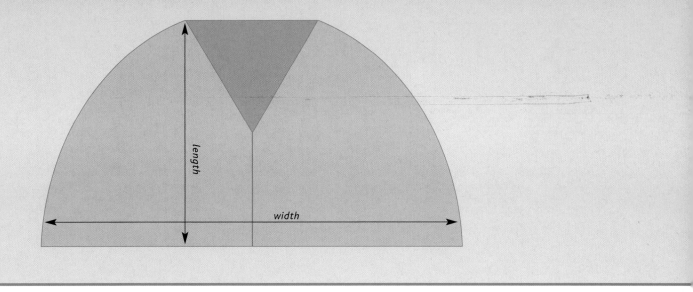

(Dec 1 st at front edge on the next row, work 3 rows straight) twice.
[20 (21:22:23:24:25) sts.]
Dec 1 st at each end of the next and 1 (1:1:3:3:3) foll 4th rows.
[16 (17:18:15:16:17) sts.]

### 1st, 2nd and 3rd sizes only
Work 1 row.
Dec 1 st at side edge on the next row.
Work 1 row.
Dec 1 st at each end of the next row.
[13 (14:15) sts.]

### All sizes
Keeping front edge straight, cont to dec 1 st at side edge on the 6 foll alt rows
[7 (8:9:9:10:11) sts], then on the next 3 rows.
[4 (5:6:6:7:8) sts.]
Work 1 row. Cast off.

## RIGHT FRONT
Work as given for Left Front, reversing shapings.

## FRONT BAND AND TIES (WORKED IN ONE PIECE)
Join side edges.
With 7 mm needles cast on 5 sts.
**Row 1:** RS. K2 * P1, k1; rep from * to last st, k1.
**Row 2:** K1 * p1, k1; rep from * to end.
Cont in rib until piece measures 34 cm (13½ in), place a marker, then cont in rib until piece fits from marker on right front to marker on left front, work a further 34 cm (13½ in). Cast off.

## TO MAKE UP
Sew side seams.
Attach ties to front edge between markers.

## LOWER EDGE
With RS facing and 7 mm needles, pick up and knit 34 (35:36:37:38:39) sts from tie round left front curve to side seam, 49 (52:54:57:59:62) sts along back, 34 (35:36:37:38:39) sts round right front curve to tie. [117 (122:126:131:135:140) sts.]
Knit 1 row. Change to 8 mm needles and cast off loosely.

## BOBBLE AND CORD (MAKE 4)
With 7 mm needles cast on 3 sts, inc in 1st st, k1, inc in last st, 5 sts, turn and purl, turn and k1, sl 1, k2tog, psso, k1, turn, p3tog. With rem st work a cord. Knit 4 rows. Fasten off.
Attach two bobble and cords to each end of front ties.

# HEADBAND
With 7 mm needles cast on 7 sts and work in rib as given for Front Band until piece reaches the desired length to fit around head. Cast off ribwise. Join seam.

*Worked in a sparkly lurex yarn, this slim-fitting sweater would look good at any special occasion teamed with trousers or skirt. It is knitted in stocking stitch with a lace garter stitch border, which is made separately and sewn on afterwards.*

# SWEATER WITH LACE COLLAR AND CUFFS

 ★★☆ EASY

*The lace pattern on the collar and cuffs requires some knitting skill.*

*Allow a little more time to complete this project as metallic yarn does take longer to work with.*

## HELPFUL HINTS
- Sew the collar to the neck edge using a firm back stitch to avoid the neckline stretching too much.

## MEASUREMENTS
### To fit bust

| | | | | | |
|---|---|---|---|---|---|
| 81 | 91 | 97 | 102 | 107 | cm |
| 32 | 34 | 36 | 38 | 40 | in |

### Actual width

| | | | | | |
|---|---|---|---|---|---|
| 75 | 81 | 85 | 91 | 96 | cm |
| 29½ | 32 | 33½ | 36 | 37¾ | in |

### Actual length

| | | | | | |
|---|---|---|---|---|---|
| 46 | 47 | 48 | 48 | 49 | cm |
| 18 | 18½ | 19 | 19 | 19¼ | in |

### Actual sleeve seam (with cuff lace edging)

| | | | | | |
|---|---|---|---|---|---|
| 46 | 49 | 49 | 49 | 49 | cm |
| 18 | 19¼ | 19¼ | 19¼ | 19¼ | in |

*In the instructions figures are given for the smallest size first; larger sizes follow in brackets. Where only one set of figures is given this applies to all sizes.*

## MATERIALS
- 14 (15:16:17:18) × 25 g balls of Rowan Lurex in Antique White Gold
- Pair each of 2¾ mm, 3¼ mm and 4 mm needles
- Stitch holder

## TENSION
29 sts and 41 rows to 10 cm (4 in) measured over stocking stitch using 3¼ mm needles.

## ABBREVIATIONS
*See page 10.*

# SWEATER

## BACK AND FRONT (ALIKE)
With 2¾ mm needles cast on 110 (118:124:132:140) sts and knit 10 rows. Change to 3¼ mm needles. Cont in st st beg with a knit row, shaping sides by dec 1 st at each end of the 5th and 5 foll 6th rows [98 (106:112:120:128) sts], then inc 1 st at each end of the 6 foll 12th rows. [110 (118:124:132:140) sts.] Cont straight until work measures 34 cm (13½ in) from beg, ending with a WS row.

### Shape raglans
Cast off 6 (6:7:7:8) sts at beg of the next 2 rows [98 (106:110:118:124) sts], then dec 1 st at each end of the next and 0 (2:4:8:12) foll alt rows [96 (100:100:100:98) sts], then on the 10 (10:10:8:7) foll 4th rows. [76 (80:80:84:84) sts.] Work 1 row, ending with a WS row.

## Shape front neck

Knit 10, turn and leave rem 66 (70:70:74:74) sts
on a st holder. Work on these sts for first side.
Cast off 4 sts at neck edge on next row. Dec
1 st at each end of the next row, then 1 st at
neck edge on the next 3 rows. Fasten off
last st.
With RS facing, rejoin yarn to centre sts. Cast
off 56 (60:60:64:64) sts and knit to end.
[10 sts.] Complete this side to match first
side, reversing shapings.

## SLEEVES (MAKE 2)

With 3¼ mm needles cast on 58
(58:64:64:66) sts. Cont in st st beg with a knit
row, shaping sides by inc 1 st at each end of
the 3rd and 2 (7:7:7:13) foll 4th rows, then on
the 17 (15:15:15:11) foll 6th rows.
[98 (104:110:110:116) sts.] Cont straight
until Sleeve measures 33 (36:36:36:36) cm
(13 (14:14:14:14) in) from beg, ending with a
WS row.

## Shape raglan

Cast off 6 (6:7:7:8) sts at beg of the next 2 rows.
[86 (92:96:96:100) sts.] Dec 1 st at each end of
the next and 20 (24:26:26:28) foll alt rows
[44 (42:42:42:42) sts], then on the 1 (0:0:0:0)
foll 4th row. [42 sts.] Work 3 rows. Cast off.

## HELPFUL HINT

*When buying lurex or glittery metallic yarns, make sure they have a polyester base as some materials will tarnish or lose their shine over time.*

## TO MAKE UP

Join 3 raglans leaving right back seam open.

### Neckband

With RS facing and 2¾ mm needles, knit up 56 (60:60:64:64) sts from back, 37 sts from top of left sleeve, 56 (60:60:64:64) sts from front, 37 sts from top of right sleeve. [186 (194:194:202:202) sts.]
Knit 9 rows. Cast off. Join remaining raglan and neckband.
Join side and sleeve seams.

### LACE FRILL NECKBAND

With 4 mm needles, cast on 25 sts and knit 1 row.
**Row 1:** Sl 1, k6, (yo, k2tog) 8 times, yo, k2.
**Rows 2, 4, 6, 8 and 10:** Knit.
**Row 3:** Sl 1, k9, (yo, k2tog) 7 times, yo, k2.
**Row 5:** Sl 1, k12, (yo, k2tog) 6 times, yo, k2.
**Row 7:** Sl 1, k15, (yo, k2tog) 5 times, yo, k2.
**Row 9:** Sl 1, k18, (yo, k2tog) 4 times, yo, k2.
**Row 11:** Sl 1, k29.
**Row 12:** Cast off 5 sts, k to end. [25 sts.]
These 12 rows form the lace edge patt.
Cont in patt until piece fits around neck edge. Do not stretch the fabric when measuring. Cast off.
Join cast-on and cast-off edges, then with RS of frill to WS body and seam to right back raglan seam, sew around neck edge firmly using a back stitch.

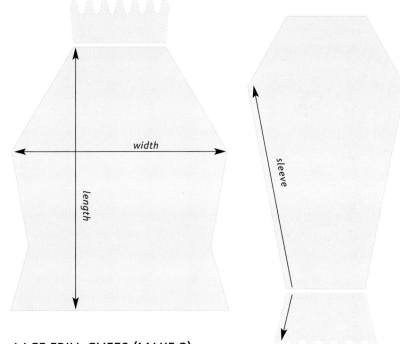

### LACE FRILL CUFFS (MAKE 2)

With 4 mm needles, cast on 25 sts and knit 1 row.
Work the 12 rows of patt as given for neckband until piece fits around cuff edge. Cast off. Join cast-on and cast-off edge, then with seam to sleeve seam, sew around cuffs edge firmly using a back stitch.

*This gorgeous bolero jacket looks fabulous over a simple black dress and is great for keeping your shoulders warm on an evening out. Using large needles and a luxurious velvety chenille yarn, it is made using simple stocking stitch.*

# BOLERO JACKET

★★☆ EASY

 *This is another simple design but requires some skill when picking up stitches around the front curves for the edges.*

*When casting off round front edges, use a large size needle as this yarn does not stretch.*

## HELPFUL HINTS

- When joining in a new ball of chenille yarn, remove approximately 5 cm (2 in) of chenille from the end of the old and beginning of the new balls by drawing the fibres between your thumbnail and index finger, leaving 5 cm (2 in) of core yarn exposed. Knot these core ends firmly together as close to the remaining chenille as possible and trim ends.
- When sewing up garments knitted in chenille yarn, use a plain yarn in a matching colour.

## MEASUREMENTS
### To fit bust

| | | | |
|---|---|---|---|
| 76–81 | 86–91 | 97–102 | cm |
| 30–32 | 34–36 | 38–40 | in |

### Actual width

| | | | |
|---|---|---|---|
| 83 | 93 | 103 | cm |
| 32¾ | 36½ | 40½ | in |

### Actual length

| | | | |
|---|---|---|---|
| 32 | 33.5 | 35 | cm |
| 12½ | 13 | 13¾ | in |

### Actual sleeve seam

46 cm
18 in

*In the instructions figures are given for the smallest size first; larger sizes follow in brackets. Where only one set of figures is given this applies to all sizes.*

## MATERIALS

- 5 (6:7) × 100 g balls of Sirdar Wow! in Raspberry Crush 758
- Pair of 7 mm needles
- 7 mm circular needle
- Stitch holder

## TENSION

8 sts and 15 rows to 10 cm (4 in) measured over stocking stitch using 7 mm needles.

## ABBREVIATIONS

*See page 10.*

# JACKET

## BACK

With 7 mm needles, cast on 33 (37:41) sts. Work 20 rows in st st beg with a knit row, ending with a WS row.

### Shape armholes

Cast off 3 sts at beg of the next 2 rows. [27 (31:35) sts.] Dec 1 st at both ends of the next 3 rows [21 (25:29) sts], then cont straight until armhole measures 19 (20.5:22) cm (7½ (8¼:8¾) in) from beg of shaping, ending with a WS row.

## Shape shoulders

Cast off 4 (5:6) sts at beg of next 2 rows.
Leave rem 13 (15:17) sts on a st holder for
back neck.

## LEFT FRONT

With 7 mm needles, cast on 8 (10:12) sts.
Cont in st st beg with a knit row. Work 1 row,
ending at front edge.

## Shape front edge

Inc 1 st at the front edge on the next 8 rows
[16 (18:20) sts], then on the foll alt row
[17 (19:21) sts], place a marker at the front
edge on the last row. Work 9 rows straight,
ending with a WS row.

## Shape armhole

Cast off 3 sts at beg of next row. [14 (16:18)
sts.] Work 1 row, then dec 1 st at armhole
edge on the next 3 rows. [11 (13:15) sts.]
Work straight until armhole measures 15 rows
shorter than Back to the shoulder, ending at
the front edge.

## Shape front neck

Cast off 2 (3:4) sts at beg of the next row
[9 (10:11) sts], then dec 1 st at neck edge on
the 5 foll alt rows. [4 (5:6) sts.] Cont straight
until Front measures the same as Back to the
shoulder, ending with a WS row. Cast off
4 (5:6) sts.

## TIES

*With 7 mm needles, cast on 2 sts, \* pass the first st made over the second. Cast on 1 st; rep from \* until ties measure approximately 25 cm (10 in), or required length. Fasten off and attach to beg of neck shaping.*

## RIGHT FRONT

Work as given for Left Front, reversing shapings.

## SLEEVES (MAKE 2)

With 7 mm needles cast on 18 (20:22) sts and purl 2 rows. Cont in st st beg with a knit row, inc 1 st at both ends of the 4 foll 15th rows. [26 (28:30) sts.] Cont straight until sleeve measures 46 cm (18 in) from beg, ending with a WS row.

## Shape sleeve top

Cast off 3 sts at beg of the next 2 rows. [20 (22:24) sts.] Dec 1 st at both ends of the 3 foll 4th rows [14 (16:18) sts], then on the 2 (3:4) foll alt rows [10 sts], then on the next 3 rows. Cast off rem 4 sts.

## TO MAKE UP

Press as instructions given on ball band. Join shoulders. Sew sleeve tops into armholes, then join side and sleeve seams.

## FRONT AND LOWER EDGES

With RS facing and 7 mm long circular needle, beg at right side seam. Knit up 19 (21:23) sts to marker on Right Front, 20 sts to beg of neck shaping, 19 sts to shoulder, knit across 13 (15:17) sts from back neck st holder, knit up 19 sts down Left Front neck edge, 20 sts to marker on Left Front, 19 (21:23) sts to side seam, 33 (37:41) sts along back edge. [162 (172:182) sts.]
Cast off loosely. Join ends. Make and attach two ties (see above).

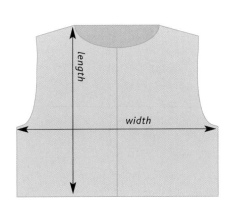

length

width

sleeve

*Feel extra special in this lovely cardigan worked in stocking stitch with an unusual ribbon yarn. A frilled edge on the front and cuffs, worked in a 4-ply cotton yarn adds extra femininity. It is tied round the waist to create a perfect fit.*

# WRAPOVER CARDIGAN

★★☆ EASY

 *The shaping at the front of the garment and the frilled edges require some knitting skill.*

## HELPFUL HINTS
- Use a firm back stitch when sewing the frill to the front edges to keep the garment in the correct shape as the main yarn is stretchy.

## MEASUREMENTS
### To fit bust
| | | | | | |
|---|---|---|---|---|---|
| 81 | 86 | 91 | 97 | 102 | cm |
| 32 | 34 | 36 | 38 | 40 | in |

### Actual width
| | | | | | |
|---|---|---|---|---|---|
| 83 | 87 | 93 | 99 | 103 | cm |
| 32½ | 34¼ | 36½ | 39 | 40½ | in |

### Actual length
| | | | | | |
|---|---|---|---|---|---|
| 48 | 49 | 50 | 51 | 52 | cm |
| 19 | 19¼ | 19½ | 20 | 20½ | in |

### Actual sleeve seam (excluding frill)
| | | | | | |
|---|---|---|---|---|---|
| 43 | 43 | 44 | 44 | 44 | cm |
| 17 | 17 | 17½ | 17½ | 17½ | in |

*In the instructions figures are given for the smallest size first; larger sizes follow in brackets. Where only one set of figures is given this applies to all sizes.*

## MATERIALS
- 9 (10:11:12:13) × 50 g balls of Rowan Cotton Braid in Renoir 353 (A)
- 2 (2:3:3:4) × 50 g balls of Rowan 4-ply Cotton in Zest 134 (B)
- Pair of 8 mm needles
- 3¼ mm long circular needle

## TENSION
10½ sts and 17 rows to 10 cm (4 in) measured over stocking stitch using 8 mm needles.

## ABBREVIATIONS
*See page 10.*

# CARDIGAN

## BACK
With 8 mm needles and A, cast on 38 (40:43:46:48) sts. Cont in st st beg with a knit row, at the same time, inc 1 st at both ends of the 9th and 2 foll 10th rows. [44 (46:49:52:54) sts.] Work a further 11 (13:13:15:15) rows straight, ending with a WS row.

### Shape armholes
Cast off 3 (3:4:4:4) sts at beg of the next 2 rows [38 (40:41:44:46) sts], then dec 1 st at both ends of the next 4 rows. [30 (32:33:36:38) sts.] Work a further 28 (28:30:30:32) rows, ending with a WS row.

### Shape shoulders
Cast off 4 sts at beg of the next 2 rows, then 3 (3:3:4:4) sts at beg of the next 2 rows. Cast off rem 16 (18:19:20:22) sts.

## LEFT FRONT

With 8 mm needles and A, cast on 34 (35:36: 38:39) sts. Cont in st st, beg with a knit row.

### Shape front edge

Work 40 (42:42:44:44) rows as follows: work 2 rows. Dec 1 st at front edge on the next and 2 foll alt rows. Work 1 row.

**Next row:** Inc 1 st at side edge and dec 1 at front edge. [31 (32:33:35:36) sts.] Dec 1 st at front edge on the 4 foll alt rows. Work 1 row.

**Next row:** Inc 1 st at side edge and dec 1 st at front edge. [27 (28:29:31:32) sts.]
Dec 1 st at front edge on the 3 (4:4:4:4) foll alt rows. Work 3 (1:1:1:1) rows.

**Next row:** Inc 1 st at side edge and dec 1 (0:0:1:1) st at front edge. Work 3 (1:1:3:3) rows. [24 (25:26:27:28) sts.]
Dec 1 st at front edge on the next and 1 (2:2:2:2) foll 4th rows.
[22 (22:23:24:25) sts.]
Work 3 rows, ending at side edge.

### Shape armhole

Cast off 3 (3:4:4:4) sts at beg of the next row and dec 1 st at end of row.
[18 (18:18:19:20) sts.] Work 1 row.
Dec 1 st at armhole edge on the next 2 rows, then dec 1 st at both ends of the next row, then 1 st at armhole edge on the next row. Keeping armhole edge straight, work 2 rows, then dec 1 st at front edge on the next and

5 (5:5:5:6) foll 4th rows until 7 (7:7:8:8) sts remain. Work straight until Front measures same as Back to beg of shoulder shaping, ending at side edge.

### Shape shoulder

Cast off 4 sts at beg of the next row. Work 1 row then cast off rem 3 (3:3:4:4) sts.

## RIGHT FRONT

With 8 mm needles and A, cast on 34 (35:36:38:39) sts. Cont in st st, beg with a purl row. Cont as given for Left Front, reversing shapings.

## SLEEVES (MAKE 2)

With 8 mm needles and A, cast on 22 (22:24:26:28) sts. Cont in st st beg with a knit row, at the same time, inc 1 st at both ends of the 7th and 6 foll 8th rows. [36 (36: 38:40:42) sts.] Cont straight until sleeve measures 43 (43:44:44:44) cm (17 (17:17½: 17½:17½) in) from beg, ending with a WS row.

### Shape sleeve top

Cast off 3 (3:4:4:4) sts at beg of the next 2 rows. [30 (30:30:32:34) sts.] Dec 1 st at both ends of the next 2 rows [26 (26:26:28: 30) sts], then on the 2 foll 4th rows [22 (22: 22:24:26) sts], then on the 2 (2:2:3:4) foll alt rows [18 sts], then on the next 4 rows. Cast off rem 10 sts.

## CUFFS (MAKE 2)

With 3¼ mm circular needle and B, cast on
121 (131:131:141:141) sts and purl 2 rows.
Cont in st st beg with a knit row and work
9 rows.

**Dec row 1:** P1, (p2tog) to end.
[61 (66:66:71:71) sts.] Work 3 rows.
**Dec row 2:** WS (K1, k2tog) to last 1 (0:0:2:2)
sts, k1 (0:0:2:2). [41 (44:44:48:48) sts.]
Knit 6 rows. Cast off.

## FRONT FRILL

With 3¼ mm circular needles and B, cast on
601 (651:651:701:701) sts and purl 2 rows.
Cont in st st beg with a knit row and work
9 rows.

**Dec row 1:** P1, (p2tog) to end.
[301 (326:326:351:351) sts.]
Work 3 rows, ending with a RS row. Cast on
41 (44:44:48:48) sts for under band.
[342 (370:370:399:399) sts.]
**Dec row 2:** WS. Knit 41 (44:44:48:48) sts,
(k1, k2tog) to last 1 (2:2:0:0) sts, k1 (2:2:0:0).
[242 (262:262:282:282) sts.]
Knit 8 rows. Cast off.

## LOWER BAND

Join shoulders. Sew sleeve tops into armholes,
then join side and sleeve seams. With 8 mm
circular needle and A, cast on 7 sts.
**Row 1:** Sl 1, k1, (p1, k1) twice, k1b.
**Row 2:** Sl 1, p1, (k1, p1) twice, k1b.

Rep these 2 rows to end until Band measures
30 cm (12 in) for the tie on the right front,
place a marker, then cont until band will fit
from shaped edge on right front around cast-
on edge on right front, back and left front with
approximately 90 cm (35 in) extra for tie. With
marker at right front slope, sew in position as
you go along, adjusting length to allow the
band to wrap around the body and tie at
the front.

## TO MAKE UP

Join short ends of cuff frills. With RS of frill to
RS of sleeve edge, position seams tog and stitch
tog. With RS of frill to WS of main body, sew frill
in position, reverse seam on under band. Fold
frill over to RS of main body and topstitch down
along the first row, worked in g st to secure.

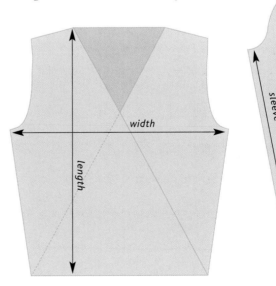

# YARN INFORMATION

**Rowan 4 Ply Cotton**: 100% cotton. 170 m/182 yd per 50 g (1¼ oz) ball.

**Rowan Biggy Print**: 100% merino wool. 30 m/33 yd per 100 g (3½ oz) ball.

**Rowan Big Wool**: 100% merino wool. 80 m/87 yd per 100 g (3½ oz) ball.

**Rowan Big Wool Tuft**: 97% merino wool, 3% nylon. 25 m/27 yd per 50 g (1¼ oz) ball.

**Rowan Chunky Cotton Chenille**: 100% cotton. 140 m/153 yd per 100 g (3½ oz) ball.

**Rowan Chunky Print**: 100% wool. 100 m/110 yd per 100 g (3½ oz) ball.

**Rowan Cork**: 95% merino wool, 5% nylon. 110 m/120 yd per 50 g (1 3/4 oz) ball.

**Rowan Cotton Braid**: 68% cotton, 22% viscose, 10% linen. 50 m/55 yd per 50 g (1¼ oz) ball.

**Rowan Cotton Glace**: 100% cotton. 115 m/126 yd per 50 g (1¼ oz) ball.

**Rowan Handknit DK Cotton**: 100% cotton. 85 m/90 yd per 50 g (1¼ oz) ball.

**Rowan Kidsilk Haze**: 70% super kid mohair, 30% silk. 210 m/229 yd per 25 g (1 oz) ball.

**Rowan Lurex Shimmer**: 80% viscose, 20% polyester. 95 m/103 yd per 25 g (1 oz) ball.

**Rowan Plaid**: 42% merino wool, 30 % acrylic fibre, 28% superfine alpaca. 100 m/110 yd per 100 g (3½ oz) ball.

**Rowan Polar**: 60% pure new wool, 30% alpaca, 10% acrylic. 100 m/110 yd per 100 g (3½ oz) ball.

**Rowan Ribbon Twist**: 70% wool, 25% acrylic, 5% polyamide. 60 m/66 yd per 100 g (3½ oz) ball.

**Rowan Summer Tweed**: 79% silk, 30% cotton. 108 m/118 yd per 50 g (1¼ oz) ball.

**Rowan Wool Cotton**: 50% merino wool, 50% cotton. 113 m/124 yd per 50 g (1¼ oz) ball.

**Rowan Yorkshire Tweed Aran**: 100% pure new wool. 160 m/175 yd per 100 g (3½ oz) ball.

**Rowan Yorkshire Tweed Chunky**: 100% pure new wool. 100 m/110 yd per 100 g (3½ oz) ball.

**Sirdar Bigga**: 50% wool, 50% acrylic. 40 m/44 yd per 100 g (3½ oz) ball.

**Sirdar Denim Chunky**: 60% acrylic, 25% cotton, 15% wool. 156 m/170 yd per 100 g (3½ oz) ball.

**Sirdar New Fizz**: 72% nylon, 19% acrylic, 9% polyester. 75 m/82 yd per 50 g (1¼ oz) ball.

**Sirdar Wow**: 100% polyester. 58 m/63 yd per 100 g (3½ oz) ball.

**Sirdar Yo-Yo**: 74% acrylic, 14% wool, 12% polyester. 800 m/874 yd per 400 g (14 oz) ball.

# SUPPLIERS AND USEFUL ADDRESSES

## UK

Rowan Yarns
Green Lane Mill
Holmfirth
West Yorkshire
HD9 2DX
Tel: (01484) 681881
Fax: (01484) 687920
Email: mail@knitrowan.com
www.knitrowan.com
*Call for details of your nearest
stockist or order online*

Sirdar Spinning Ltd
Flanshaw Lane
Alverthorpe
Wakefield
West Yorkshire
WF2 9ND
Tel: (01924) 371501
Fax: (01924) 290506
Email: orders@sirdar.co.uk
www.sirdar.co.uk
*Call for details of your nearest
stockist or order online*

## USA

Knitting Fever Inc.
PO Box 502
Roosevelt
New York 11575
Tel: (516) 546 3600
Fax: (516) 546 6871
Email:
webmaster@knittingfever.com
*Stockist of Sirdar yarns*

Rowan USA
4 Townsend West
Suite 8
Nashua
New Hampshire 03064
Tel: (603) 886 5041/5043
Email wfibers@aol.com
*Call for details of your nearest
stockist*

## AUSTRALIA

Australian Country Spinners
314 Albert Street
Brunswick
Victoria 3056
Tel: (03) 9380 3888
*Stockist of Rowan yarns*

Creative Images
PO Box 106
Hastings
Victoria 3915
Australia
Tel: (03) 5979 1555
Fax: (03) 5979 1544
Email:
creative@peninsula.starway.net.au
*Stockist of Sirdar yarns*

## SOUTH AFRICA

Arthur Bales Ltd
62 4th Avenue
Linden
Johannesburg 2195
Tel: (027) 118 882 401
Fax: (027) 117 826 137
Email: Arthur@new.co.za
*Stockist of Rowan yarns*

Saprotex International (Pty)
PO Box 1293
East London 5200
Tel: (027) 43 763 1551
Fax: (027) 43 763 1929
Email: tbarratt@bertrand.co.za
*Stockist of Sirdar yarns*

# INDEX

## ACKNOWLEDGEMENTS

I would like to thank all those involved in the creation of this book, especially to Rosemary Wilkinson and Clare Sayer for their continued support and organisation. Thank you to Sian Irvine for her lovely photographs, models Emma, Jo, Kat, Natalie and Sarah and Isobel Gillan for her design.

Special thanks go to the pattern checker Marilyn Wilson. Also to David Rawson and Pauline Brown at Sirdar, and Linda Parkhouse and all at Rowan, who helped to sort out the yarn requirements. A huge thank you to both Sirdar and Rowan for producing such lovely yarns, which help to inspire all the garments I design. And where would I be without my loyal knitters, Margaret Craik, Helen Hawe, Thelma Seager, Irene Hall and Christine D'Acunzo? Who always amaze me by their speed and efficiency to turn garments around, even at the busiest times of the year.

I shall always be indebted to the magazines and spinners who commission my designs and who have now become special people in my life. Especially Elena Costella and Allison Stewart who work for the D C Thompson group of magazines and Margaret Maino and Beth Johnson from Creative Plus Publishing Ltd.

I have to thank my family for getting my interest in knitting going in the first place, and also for putting up with being surrounded by wool for all these years, and my artistic temperament!

A very special thank you to my daughter Sarah, who soon became proficient in the skill, and helped with the knitting in this book, and to Robert my son, because he's my son. I suppose they will always have this image of their mum with knitting needles and wool.